To Callum
all the best

This book is dedicated to my father Samuel Campbell Mason who died on 28th November 2018. He would have loved to have made this trip. He was there in spirit.

My thanks to Jenny Slaven for checking Spelling and Grammar. I'm a biker who writes not a writer who bikes.

The Build Up and Preparation

"What now?" I wondered to myself, having ridden from Argentina to Alaska.

Get a job and act like a normal person.

My decision to resign from my job and spend four and a half months of my time out riding the Americas had depleted my funds and asked a lot of the ones I love.

It had been quite an adjustment to come back to normality. Being on the road with no other plan than to get a little further north each day had been an immensely freeing experience. For the first time in my adult life I had no work to go to, and at times did not even know what day or date it was. Of course, there were challenges and frustrations but, as with all travels, time just made them the fabric of the trip.

I made the adjustment and got myself a good job in a good company with some great new workmates and life returned to what might be considered normal. I became a Glasgow to Edinburgh commuter.

Saying that, I don't believe a "trip of a lifetime" should be viewed as a singular event, that's far too limiting, and I knew I had more to do. The question now was where and when and how. The answer to where was easy. I had ridden from the bottom to the top of the world, and now I wanted to ride around it. The when was more difficult, as that was linked to the equally difficult how.

My outline plan was to ride through Russia, Kazakhstan and Mongolia, then back into Russia, ending up at Vladivostok. From there I could take a ferry to South Korea, then airfreight the bike and myself to Vancouver. I could then ride across Canada and the USA ending up on the east coast. I researched and pondered all of this for a while. The obstacles were clear based on learnings from my last trip; time away from family, post trip readjustment and cost. This trip would take at least three months and the costs of flights and bike transport were looking very steep. There had to be another way.

The other way presented itself to me one dark winter evening when I was listening to Adventure Rider Radio. There was an advert for a company named Rusmototravel doing tours from Moscow to Vladivostok. I checked out the website and liked what I saw. The problem was that I did not want to go on a guided trip and the route was only travelling through Russia. I could drop Kazakhstan but, for me, Mongolia was non-negotiable. There were some gems of information on Alex's website, for example, his trip lasted four weeks and he rail freighted the bikes back to Moscow. If you don't ask you don't get, I decided, and wrote to Alex with a proposal. It went along the lines of:

"Hey Alex can I meet you in Moscow, ride with you to the north-west corner of Mongolia then do my own thing?"

Then adding:

"Can you also arrange transport for Boris (my bike) from Vladivostok back to Moscow and keep it there for me until I pick it up?"

It seemed logical to me. I would enjoy the solo trip to Moscow. Alex would lead a group, including me, through the allegedly duller part of the route. His knowledge of the roads and sights would transform that section of the trip plus it would give me, and my family, confidence by easing me into the Russian experience. Just as important, I would be able to get my bike back to Moscow for a reasonable price then ride it home.

Time away would be reduced by splitting the trip in two, as I would do the Americas later. Post trip adjustment would be transformed by the shorter length of the trip, meaning I could probably get a lifestyle break from work. Cost was looking much more attractive too.

Alex's response was perfect. He was more than happy for me to accompany him for part of his trip and was also willing to arrange bike transportation, pick up and storage for Boris. The plan was in motion.

My first trip and book, *Ride to the Midnight Sun,* was all about being able to have an adventure in two weeks and one day, no need for life changing decisions such as giving up work and stressing relationships. My second major trip and book, *Llama's Bananas and Bears,* was a four-and-a-half-month Pan American adventure and did involve life-changing decisions. What I was planning to do now was somewhere in between and potentially a more realistic proposition for people trying to balance real world commitments with a desire to circumnavigate the planet.

Various emails flowed between Moscow and Lenzie, and a final plan and cost was agreed. Alex sent me the following itinerary:

20th May 2018 – Meet up in Moscow

21st May 2018 - Moscow

22nd May 2018 - Moscow

23rd May 2018 – Nizhny Novgorod

24th May 2018 - Kazan

25th May 2018 – Izhevsk

26th May 2018 - Yekaterinburg

27th May 2018 - Yekaterinburg

28th May 2018 - Tumen

29th May 2018 - Omsk

30th May 2018 - Novosibirsk

I now started planning the remainder of my trip around that. From previous experience I was clear on my ferry route, Newcastle to Amsterdam overnight. Not too far to ride and the destination has great connectivity into Germany and beyond. The original route I had in mind was to continue through Poland, Belarus and onwards to Moscow but I hadn't realised that Belarus was not in the EU; it would therefore involve a visa. I adjusted the plan to route through Poland, Lithuania, Latvia into Russia.

After leaving Alex in Novosibirsk I would ride around 700 miles south to the Tashanta border crossing into Mongolia. My route through Mongolia would initially take me south to Altai, then north and central; this seemed to be a favourite of recent adventurers. I would then head north from the capital city of Ulaanbaatar to the allegedly modern Russian city of Ulan-Ude, before heading east through Siberia to my final destination, Vladivostok.

Visas would be required for Russia (triple entry) and Mongolia. The Russian tourist visa options were unsuitable as you could only get a double entry, valid in total for just 30 days. That would be too risky in terms of time. The other option, multi entry business, was expensive at around £400 but it looked like an unavoidable spend. Alex could help me with a tourist visa but I would probably have to get a broker such as RealRussia to arrange the business one.

Required vaccinations were Hepatitis A and Tetanus, both of which were up to date from my previous trip, so that was a cost saving.

Other documentation seemed relatively straightforward; driving licence, passport and V5. I did not see any mention of an international driving licence but I thought I might get one just in case and I needed to arrange Russian and Mongolian motorcycle insurance. Russia seemed easily available at border crossings but Mongolia still needed further research. I would also need Travel cover which I would likely get from Navigator as they offered specific packages for motorcyclists.

My trusty 2009 BMW R1200GS Boris had been refurbished after the last big trip using a mix of new and used parts by *Racin and Cruisin Motorcycles* in Kirkintilloch where Craig and his son Cee-Jay operate an old-style bike shop providing personal quality service. They did a great job of restoring Boris to his shiny best, considering he was approaching 60,000 miles. I trusted them to help me prepare for this new adventure. Preparation would take place around April 2018 and would include a nuts and bolts check, full service and a shaft dive refurb.

Boris was already adventure ready, with upper and lower crash bars, indestructible Bumot Panniers, Weber front and rear shocks, Touratech Fog Lights and a BMW Top Case. I had a Garmin Zumo Sat Nav which would see me through the EU, but was still researching what I might do in Russia. There are free downloadables that my friends Raymond and Hutch had used on the Pan American trip but they had not worked on my older unit. I thought I might buy a Russian SIM card and use Google Maps. With that in mind I purchased a really neat phone mount from SP Connect.

I was also in very good shape for gear with a tent, sleeping bag, bike gear etc already in place, so no real expenses there. On return from the Pan American trip I had replaced my beat-up BMW suit with a Rukka one and my crash damaged Shark helmet with a Schubert E1 Flip Up Adventure style. I had witnessed the sun shading benefit the skip provided for my two amigos on our last trip. My original Sidi Adventure boots were still in decent shape and had proven their worth.

In July 2017 my boss was changing at work, prompting me to announce my plans and ask for time off. I explained my plans, requesting a six-week break starting 14th May 2018. I would take three weeks holiday and three weeks leave of absence - the three weeks holiday to include a week carried from the previous year. As a biker and a lover of travel herself she was supportive and thankfully my incoming boss was too. The fact that I would raise money for Deafblind Scotland helped with the sell!

Last time around we put ourselves out there quite a bit in our bid to help raise funds for a new purpose-built centre for Deafblind Scotland a few hundred yards from my home. This included attending events, local TV slots and quite a number of post trip presentations. In the end we raised £6,700 against a finger in the air target of £10,000. We were pleased to work with and help this brilliant charity supporting amazing people. This time around, with it being a solo trip I decided to make it lower key; though I would not be chasing publicity, I was happy to do what I could, posting trip presentations and hoping that I could get us closer to the original £10,000.

I may come across as organised and sorted, but I can assure you I am not. Well maybe I am kind of organised, but definitely not sorted! Doing stuff like this has led me to a lot of whys and what ifs, constant questions in my head - often in the middle of the night.

There have been many times when I've thought, stay at home, do something different, don't put yourself out there - but not for long. I have a map in our spare bedroom with black lines drawn showing the Nordkapp and Pan American routes. I often look at it and plot the route with my finger around the world. It just feels like something I have to do.

Another interesting development is my 'adventure rider industry' fatigue. It has become such a huge industry with products, Facebook full of trips, endless rallies and events, magazines, TV, Radio etc. With all of that activity comes mini celebrities, and with that, competition, resulting in lots of opinionated people dictating how it should be done. I can hear you saying, pot calling the kettle black there, and you may have a point. I wanted to do my trip; I wanted to write about it and I would create a personal Facebook group to allow those who were interested to take a look. I won't tell you this is how it should be done and I'm not chasing followers.

I took a big financial step in October 2017 with the booking of my flights. I booked an Aeroflot flight from Vladivostok to Moscow on 21st of June and a Moscow to Glasgow flight on the 22nd. My return to Moscow to pick up Boris was booked for the 12th of July. I also reserved an Airport hotel for the night of the 21st of June. The Vlad flight cost £172 and the Moscow – Glasgow ones were supplemented with air miles reducing it to £70.

During October I took a late season ride up to one of my favourite places, Applecross in Wester Ross, set in a spectacular location looking onto the isles of Raasay and Skye. Access is either by a spectacular single lane mountain pass called the Bealach na Bà (Pass of the cattle) or a winding coastal road. The jewel in the crown is the fine sea food and real ale served at the Applecross Inn. The ride up was great, with mainly dry weather and fuelled by a breakfast stop at the Green Welly in Tyndrum. I was with Big Tree, Hutch and Kenny, a friend of Hutch. Big Tree has been a lifetime friend and recently got back into bikes. Hutch is also a lifetime friend and rode the Pan American highway with me. Kenny who is just returning to biking will, I am sure, be a friend from now on. We rented a couple of Wigwams as we knew the wet weather was coming. We had a cracking night with brilliant food and lots of laughs in the pub that night.

Now here's a thing. I had a completely different set of emotions towards my planned trip versus the last one. Building up to the last one, all I wanted to do was discuss it. It was 90% excitement and 10% apprehension. This time I felt the opposite. Hutch asked me how I was feeling about the trip and I could not end the conversation soon enough.

I think the main reason was that I was travelling solo and that Russia had not had great press recently. Not talking too much about it helped me feel calmer.

I had been doing a bit of googling about Garmin Russia maps and came up with an eBay company selling them for £28. I would most definitely get a Russian phone sim but the Garmin maps also seemed worthwhile. After a check that I could change my unit to a Cyrillic keyboard for typing in destinations, the order was placed. My search for a Mongolia map yielded no results so I ended up downloading a free version from *openstreetmaps,* which on paper looked good. The process was simple:

- ✓ Log on to the website
  http://garmin.openstreetmap.nl/
- ✓ Select Mongolia
- ✓ Request a down load
- ✓ You receive a confirmation mail then a mail with a link
- ✓ Click on the link
- ✓ Go to Glasgow (in my case) and buy a micro SD and holder
- ✓ Insert it in the computer
- ✓ Create a folder "Garmin" in the Micro SD
- ✓ Drag the file across
- ✓ Put the Micro SD in the Garmin
- ✓ Power it on
- ✓ Select the country
- ✓ Wow

Looked like it worked. It will be interesting to provide feedback on the road between this versus the paid versions.

The Russian SD Card took some time but finally arrived. There was no Garmin packaging as such so I guess it was 'created' somehow. I plugged it in and searched for Russia or what might be Russia in Cyrillic but could only find a list of various Cyrillic names which totally confused me. I messaged the seller who confirmed which one was Russia, after which all seemed good. I asked what the others were, but his reply was lost in translation! I later confirmed with a Russian guy at work that it included various nearby countries such as Latvia, Ukraine etc. I would only be able to find out how good it was once I was on the road. As a back-up I used the same process described above to add a free version of Russia to my Mongolian SD card. It would be ironic if that's how my paid one was created.

In November I decided I would start booking up some accommodation for the first few days after leaving Alex. I booked three hotels using Booking.com. One was in Gorno-Altaysk, a day's drive south, another near the border and a final one in Olgiy in Mongolia. The idea was to ensure I had accommodation and targets on that first solo part of my trip, and would get safely over the border. I received a nice email from the proprietor of the hotel just inside the Russian border, advising me their place needed special paperwork and was down a 27-kilometre dirt track with a deep river crossing. She said they were opening a hotel in town (no special paperwork or river crossing). I took her advice and cancelled my booking, saying I would get back to her nearer the time. I also decided to book Alex's recommended Azimut hotel in Vladivostok for the final three nights.

I booked my ferry trip from Newcastle to Amsterdam at a cost of £343 and Navigator Travel Insurance (Motorcycle Gold) at £165. The only big upfront expense left now was visas, which I would look at in the new year.

November also brought some sad news; MotoScotland was to close. MotoScotland had provided our off-road training before the Pan American trip and I loved what Clive and Donna were doing up in Inveraray. So much hard work and passion over their five years of operation. I messaged Clive to wish Donna and him all the best for the future.

December blew in a tough ending to 2017 with my 86-year-old father being admitted to hospital with a chest infection which resulted in him moving in and out of a delirious state. My 83-year-old Mother was not helping by refusing to accept she was incapable of taking care of him without help. January saw my father moving back home and a return to a form of normality.

They took some but not all of the care offered, leaving us to just wait and see. I am always conscious of their age and the possible implications related to my longer-term travel plans, especially the need to deal with any events, should they occur while I'm away. But I won't let the possibility stop me getting out there. Does that sound selfish? Maybe it is, maybe I have to be, for me.

My next bike related decision was on tyres. I had a dilemma as I had worked out several options:

1. Run my current part worn TCK70's to Moscow then change them to Anakee Wild's
   - o + Good use of current tyres and Alex would help me arrange the change
   - o – New tyres may not last the entire trip
2. Fit Heidenau K60 Scouts and run them for the whole journey
   - o + Minimum hassle, no need to carry or change tyres
   - o – Not great reputation in the wet and would be well worn by the end of the trip
3. Fit Metzeler Tourance and ride to the edge of Mongolia and change to Anakee Wild's
   - o + Road orientated for the tarmac part of the trip and off-road orientated for   Mongolia
   - o - Expensive and having to carry and change tyres

In the end I opted for option 3. Although it was expensive, I decided it was the safest option. I managed to track down a BMW dealer in Novosibirsk, a perfect location for both a tyre and oil change. I contacted Alex who confirmed he would help me arrange this. This would be on the last day I would spend with the group, so it seemed right that I would be heading off with the bike checked and shod for the solo part of the journey.

February saw me order my six Month Multi Entry Russian Visa from Real Russia visa services. The only difficulty in the application process was having to list entry and exit dates for every stamp in my passport. I had never counted them before, but the Argentina to Alaska trip consisted of 26 international border crossings, ten of which were between Argentina and Chile. So theoretically this trip with only four border crossings should be a breeze?

March 11th 2018 – nine weeks to departure. Into single figures at last. I can only describe the feeling by now as scary excitement. I expected these feelings to increase in intensity as time moved on.

After getting agreement from Hutch and Raymond, I got our Deafblind Scotland Just Giving page - https://www.justgiving.com/fundraising/thelongwayuppanameri can - up-to-date and add in my own trip. In that way I hoped we could edge closer to our original target of £10,000. I would hold back from publicising it until much nearer the departure date.

I noticed Alex from Rusmototravel was still offering places on our tour, while the July one had sold out, and wondered if there could be a chance of it being cancelled. I felt sure even if it was, Alex would take care of me.

My Russian business invitation letter was due on March 13th which just happened to coincide with an announcement by the British Prime Minister accusing Russia of using chemical weapons in an attempt to murder a defected Russian spy and his daughter. It was a horrible situation with both the father, daughter and a policeman seriously ill in hospital. I received a message from Real Russia saying my invitation letter was delayed but they could not give a reason. It made me nervous. Theresa May gave the Russian government until Midnight on March 14th to confess or explain how they had lost a nerve agent. Russia immediately denied any involvement and ignored the deadline. So, on March 15th the UK expelled twenty-three Russian diplomats and banned Harry and William (the Royals) from going to the world cup. On that same day Real Russia called to say my invitation letter would be with them on the Thursday. The documents arrived ok, so I set a date of March 27th based on cheap flights to go down to London and get my finger prints etc done. During discussion with a very helpful Lina in Real Russia, she suggested they process the Mongolian visa first, then I would have both visas available on the same day. This led to some frantic activity in applying, printing, completing and sending a pack of stuff that day. Royal Mail did their job and Lina confirmed on the Friday that she had all she needed to proceed.

BBC news reported the government had issued a 'be aware' warning to UK citizens travelling to Russia. Apparently, the Russian media were stirring up an anti-British furore. Hopefully it would be yesterday's news in eight weeks' time.

Did you just order one tyre? The message flashed up in front of me on my phone at work.

No, I replied, *I ordered four.*

Well, one has just arrived. An hour later I received a text to say another had arrived. Bizarre, very bizarre I thought. Moto-Tyres and DPD are doing something wrong here. When I arrived home, I identified the two as the Metzeler Torrance's, it seemed the Anakee Wilds were in the Netherlands. They did in fact arrive together the next day. Now there were four.

Visa anxiety continued with a phone call from Real Russia to inform me that, due to worsening relationships, the Russian Embassy had informed them that visas would take at least twenty working days to process rather than five. This would still be ok if it actually was just twenty days, it would take delivery out to the end of April. But with Bank Holidays in May it did not leave much further margin for error.

I had been thinking that I needed to start my journey from the Atlantic west coast in Scotland and end it at the Atlantic east coast in the USA to complete my ride around the world. I had considered leaving from Ayr where I used to live, ending in Boston, where I used to visit for work.

I mentioned to wee Gary at work that I was heading up to a Rally at Sunart Campsite in Strontian and that we would be riding out to Ardnamurchan Point.

"You do know that's the most westerly point on the Scottish mainland" he said.

The most westerly point in Scotland to the most easterly point in the USA, I thought, asking Gary to Google the most easterly point on mainland USA. It came up as Sail Rock, east of West Quoddy Head in Maine.

"Look they both have lighthouses" he said. "Lighthouse to Lighthouse!"

With that new information, I decided my official trip start would be on Saturday 28th of April at Ardnamurchan Point. I would stay flexible on my finishing point as Boston was still in the running.

On Tuesday 27/3 I headed down to London to submit the visa. I had a problem free flight down, and on arrival checked out the location of the Russian Visa Centre. It was a twenty-minute walk from Liverpool Street Station so that worked perfectly. First priority when reaching the station was to get some breakfast. I still cannot believe how expensive London is, with a very basic breakfast costing £15. Lina had told me to call her if I arrived early as she could maybe pull the appointment forward, freeing me up for the rest of the day. I did not get Lina but another lady advised me that she could pull it in from 2pm to 12 noon.

I was just about to head towards the Visa Centre when my phone rang. It was Lina.

"Hi Mr Mason, we received the wrong type of visa from Mongolia. They gave you a Tourist visa rather than an Auto Tourist visa. I am having it re-issued but it might not be back for 12 noon."

Visa anxiety swept over me in a flash. What if they did not get it back today? I agreed with Lina that I would target the original 2pm time and that she would let me know if there was an issue. I decided to go locate the Visa centre anyway, then find something to do around there.

I enjoyed the walk, following directions on my phone and finally came upon the Visa centre located in a little back lane in the Barbican area of London. I noticed it closed at 3pm, not leaving me with much leeway if there was a problem. Heading off down a nearby busy street I started to kill the two hours I had left.

After ten minutes or so I came across the Museum of London. Result! I thought. Warm, dry, seating, exhibits and free. I spent my time wandering around, then watching some downloads on my iPad. I was still concerned though, constantly checking my phone for messages.

I started thinking about plan B if the Mongolian visa was late. I was still on holiday tomorrow so worst case I could stay over and that would buy us another day. Hotels were around £100 and a return flight £250, so it was not an attractive proposition but I might have no other choice.

Around 1:30pm I decided to call Lina, fearing the worst, to see if there was an update.

" Hi Mr Mason" she said, "we have your passport and we are all good for 2pm".

A wave of relief swept through me as I headed out of the museum and back towards the Visa centre. I arrived 10 minutes early and within 5 minutes a guy approached me.

"Mr Mason?" he enquired

"Yes, that's me I responded".

He explained the process. I should take my documents, walk through the white door, pass security then wait my turn. They would keep my documents and there was nothing to pay. I shook his hand, thanked him and walked through the white door. A security guard checked me over in a friendly manner then handed me a ticket number, 218. I sat there watching the five or so open kiosk's processing people. Within 15 minutes or so my number flashed up and I moved up to the kiosk. The process went smoothly, with the lady checking my documents then fingerprinting me. Within 5 minutes I was walking back out through the door, feeling good.

I considered taking the subway down to the Embankment but my old work Oyster Card had finally expired. As I pondered what to do, I got a text from my daughter Stephanie.

It said "Hi Grampa" complete with a picture of a developing baby. My first grandchild.

This was not 'new news' but she had wanted to keep it a secret until her 12-week check and now it was public knowledge. I felt elated and ditched my plans to go into the centre, choosing instead to go to a traditional London pub to celebrate. From then on, the remainder of the day went pub, shops, pub, haircut, food and pub!

Next day while I was out, I booked Boris in with *Racin and Cruisin Motorcycles* for his pre-trip preparation. I explained to the owner Craig that I had created 'Craig's list'.

Craig's List:

- Full Service
- Replace Brake Pads Front and Rear
- Check/Replace wheel bearings
- Adjust valves
- Fit Tyres
- Fit USB Charger
- Fit brighter bulbs to spotlights
- Full nuts and bulbs check
- Order extra oil and air filter

I was aware Craig could not make Boris bullet-proof but I knew he would do his best.

I finalised my post Alex hotel bookings in Gorna-Altaysk and Kosch-Agatsch near the Mongolian border. I cancelled my one Mongolian reservation and booked hotels for the next Russian-Siberian leg of the trip. This was except for between Chita and Blagoveshchensk where there was only an un-bookable roadhouse. Alex helped with recommendations and all the hotels could be cancelled at short notice. A bit of me thought this was too pre-planned but if offered me a feeling of comfort, particularly as I would be on my own.

During my last trip, Hutch and I arrived late into an overflowing campsite in British Columbia. We had tried and failed to find a spot when an enthusiastic young man came up asking if we wanted to share his pitch with his two friends. It turned out to be a very tight and bumpy spot, but we were very grateful. We had a good night by the campfire and Kevin Chow explained how he longed for adventure too. He worked as a Marketing Manager at a large Harley Davidson dealer, however his choice of steed was an immaculate GS1200. During that night Kevin arranged a camping spot further north at his aunt's house in Quesnel and invited us to stay with him in Vancouver on our way home. He also helped me by removing one of his top-box mounting bolts to replace a missing one in Boris.

We took up Kevin's offers of hospitality and both his Aunts (Signe) garden campsite and his Vancouver home were a delight to visit. A few years later Kevin realised his dream and set off on an around the world trip on that same GS1200 (https://worldoverlan.ca). Kevin recently blogged about useful apps for the traveller, so based on that I downloaded two of them. *Maps me* is a downloadable mapping application which you can use as a route finder on your phone without data. I also downloaded *iOverlander* which I had used before but not in earnest. Both apps link together and look very useful indeed. As an example, I mentioned there was only an un-bookable roadhouse between Chita and Blagoveshchensk. I managed to locate Erofey Palich in *iOverlander* and see some details such as, a quiet camping area behind it. When I linked it to *Maps me*, I could see a reasonably detailed lay out of it. Kevin is the gift that just keeps on giving.

The week of April 15th brought two major steps forward. The first and the most important was the arrival of my passport complete with Russian and Mongolian visas. Real Russia had delivered a little earlier than expected. The other was the collection of a fully serviced Boris. I took him out for a spin that night and he was running like a sweetie. In the same week I also received a trip launch email from Alex introducing the group and providing useful travel information. The group would be made up of Alex lead, another Alex as a second guide, two Germans, two Canadians, a Dutchman and an English guy.

I mentioned before I had been feeling 10% excitement and 90% apprehension. Now the pendulum was swinging, I would put it at 70% excitement and 30% apprehension.

With Visa's safely in place I decided it was time to launch my Facebook group and advise the people I deal with at work that I would be heading off. Although I did not want an 'all over Facebook' thing going on, having received several requests for a blog, I found this to be the easiest way. I made the group private and, in that way (I thought) I could invite my close family and friends and add anyone who asked for a blog. Facebook's definition of private is if you invite anyone, they can invite their friends also so before I knew it I had over 100 members. Not what I had intended but there was no decent way back. It's not that I didn't want people to take an interest. I guess I just felt vulnerable. What if I screwed it up?

On Friday 27th April I set off to the Sunart Wildcat Rally. I headed through Glasgow and after crossing the Erskine Bridge noticed what looked like Tree a few vehicles in front. I pulled up beside him at the first set of lights and greeted him in a "how are you big sox" Scottish way. We were due to meet at the Green Welly further north but decided we would ride on to the petrol station in Glen Coe village. The ride north was problem free and as spectacular as ever. We fuelled up as planned and a few miles later took the short hop across Loch Linnhe on the Corran Ferry. On arrival at the Sunart campsite we saw Hutch and Kenny's tents with their panniers protecting a spot for us. They both arrived from a ride out as we were pitching up. Kenny was riding a brand-new Triumph Tiger 800 and was rightfully as proud as punch. It was a cracking night as we wandered down to the local hotel to sup a few beers overlooking the bay. It was so nice we ended up eating outside. Another of those special moments enjoying the view, sunshine, real ale and banter. We headed back to the campsite and sampled various whiskies by the fire before retiring to our tents.

We all woke up after a very cold nights sleep with temperatures dipping to minus 4c. It was a take it easy morning with a walk, breakfast at the local café and some chilling out. We picked up our Rally t-shirts and purchased some raffle tickets from Mike the organiser. The Rally was small and friendly which was perfect for us.

At lunchtime we headed off to Ardnamurchan Lighthouse, the official starting point for my trip. It was a spectacular ride on single track coastal roads. After an hour or so we finally arrived at our destination. Ardnamurchan Lighthouse is located on the most western point of mainland UK with spectacular views of the small isles and Skye. It was a perfect choice as a starting point. The lads gave me some celebrity treatment by taking lots of photos and we chatted to some tourists looking on. I had a moment of reflection as I gazed out to sea, imagining reaching my final end-point some 3,000 miles across the ocean. I felt calm and happy.

Contemplating the ride ahead at Ardnamurchan Point - Scotland

Let the Trip begin

On Saturday 28th of April with 59,552 miles on the clock, Boris and I commenced the "Once around the block" trip. It was a brief ride down to the village of Kilchoan where we stopped off for a coffee and were served by a very friendly lady from Santiago in Chile. We exchanged stories and sipped our coffee out in the sun. The ride back to Sunart was even better than the ride out although the weather was looking a lot cloudier and rain was on its way. There was a Rally barbecue that night where we all mingled and enjoyed the goings on. We were all off to bed early after the raffle which yielded me a nice bottle of red wine.

We were up early and raring to go on Sunday and arrived at Ardgour half an hour before the first ferry was due. We decided to take a longer loop home via Oban and Inveraray but first a breakfast spot had to be discovered. We called in at a hotel where a friendly person recommended the Castle Stalker View Café further down the road. It turned out to be a brilliant recommendation as we all agreed it was a top-class breakfast. Our next agreed stopping point was Inveraray and the ride there was just great. Super scenery, a mixture of damp and dry roads and all bikes were on song. We all said our farewells in Inveraray and headed home at our own pace.

Sunday 13/05/18

It had been a week of restless sleeps and early awakenings and this was no different. It was 5am as I peeked out of the curtains at a wet morning. It was only last week I had been full of praise for weather forecasters accuracy these days. Dry in the West and wet in the East was the undelivered promise. Still, I would see plenty of rain on my journey I'm sure.

I felt a sense of calm as I made my way to the shower. I think it was that be in control, calm thing I can do when I am anxious. I pulled on some casual clothes, had some coffee and got straight into packing. I had decided to pack lighter than the last trip forgoing the big 40 litres Lomo bag I had strapped to my seat. That made quite a difference in usable space. "Aye 40 litres" I can hear you say. I had messed around with what and where I would put things in my available space, so I knew what I was doing.

I opened the garage door quietly so as not to disturb Amber sleeping above. First job was a tyre pressure check. That's always stressful, as I had come out to a flat many years ago on the morning of a trip across to Ireland. Then it was a case of loading the bike. I was ready, but way too early.

I drove up to the local shop and picked up some lip cream then returned and cooked some breakfast. Amber came down around 8am, which was early for her on a Sunday. It was hard to describe the atmosphere between us. Tense, anxious, with a layer of calm. She was not comfortable with the solo part of this trip.

The weather started to clear so I wheeled Boris out into the driveway. I strapped my tyres on to the seat propped against the top box. I had talked about leaving between 10 and 11am and it was still only 9:30am. I was ready to go. I asked Amber to take a few pictures and then hugged her and we said our goodbyes. I was off.

The roads were drying out and the sun was shining as I took the familiar route towards work but this time, I exited onto the M73 as I was heading south. The ride down was good and Boris was comfortable and running well. I crossed the border into England and considered stopping at a rest area with a Costa Coffee, but decided to ride on. I exited onto the A69 towards Newcastle and kept my eye out for a good coffee stop. I then remembered doing the same thing on my "Ride to the Midnight Sun" trip and then, as now, there was nothing. I decided to pull into a lay-by for a stretch and to check the security of the tyres. As I pulled in, I noticed about five guys all standing peeing outside a minibus, I rode on.

Next lay-by was empty and clean, so I stopped there. The tyres were secure so after a brief rest I rode on. I finally entered Newcastle and followed the signs to the ferry. I pulled into a services area for fuel and picked up a Snickers bar as contingency food. There was a Burger King but it looked uninviting, as did the whole area. I rode on down to the ferry terminal and noticed a Brewers Fayre nearby. I parked up and went in only to find it mobbed with families all plundering a buffet. Not for me.

I rode down to the loading area and was third in the queue behind two German bikers. I smiled and greeted them and got stuck into my Snickers bar. They had been on a tour of Scotland and had loved it. The queue started to grow quickly with probably 50 or so bikes lined up. I was repacking my top box with what I thought was plenty of time to go when a guy waved us forward. It led to a frantic repack and as it was a short distance, I pushed the bike forward. I felt organised and handed over a copy of my booking. "Passport please" said the lady. That resulted in me rummaging through my pockets and handing it over. She convinced me to pre-pay for the buffet, which I had resisted but it was apparently the only show in town. I paid up then decided to push my bike a few yards and sort stuff out. As I pushed it down the slope, I realised I could not operate the front brake as I was holding my documents. I managed to stop it but only just. That would have been embarrassing!

I passed through another check of tickets and passport and soon I was onboard. They had already handed out tie down straps, which me and my two German friends had mastered of sorts. Boris was tight against the ferry wall and with two straps, was well secured. "Right just need my bag now," I thought, only to discover the overnight bag was in the pannier jammed against the wall. Thankfully there were plenty of people around, so I unstrapped Boris and lifted him upright while a big Dutch bloke wrestled the bag out.

I made my way upstairs to my cabin and felt relatively relaxed. I had a beer up on the sun deck observing the various Dutch stag parties on their way home. They were boisterous but bearable. I then made my way down for the 5pm buffet session. The secret of the Buffet is to go at off-peak times when it's quiet and the food is fresh. It was actually good.

I had a quiet night with a further couple of beers listening to a country and western singer in the bar followed by a downloaded movie in my cabin. The movie was Titanic II which I thought would be appropriate. It was awful, time to sleep.

Monday 14/05/18

I had a great sleep in that little cabin, rocked gently by the motion of the ship. I organised my gear then headed out to the onboard Starbucks coffee shop for pastries and a large Americana, which was bliss! I wandered around outside staring into the fog and enjoying the fresh air in my face. Before I knew it, it was time to head down to the car deck to get ready for the off. I had a master plan to tie the bag temporarily to the back rather than getting someone to help me wrestle it into the pannier. Not quite straightforward but I managed to get it held on long enough to survive getting off the ship. The swarm of bikes all rolled off into the bright Dutch sunshine and almost all pulled over to the side to make some adjustments to luggage etc.

Soon I was on my way east. Next ocean would be the Pacific. My badly out of date Sat Nav maps started to let me down very early and soon I was lost. I pulled over and stripped off my bike jacket as it was getting very hot. I took my time checking on google maps for a route and mounted my phone for the off. I removed the lining from my jacket and switched to my summer gloves. The phone nav was unreadable in the sun and the volume was too low on the voice instructions, so not much help. Between the Sat Nav and the phone, I finally got onto the A1 East. It was a busy, fast road and I took some breaks at service stations as I made my way to Germany. I wanted to get to the other side of Hanover before stopping.

At around 5pm I finally pulled into a service station east of Hanover with a view to eating and finding a place for the night. The eating was easy as there was a snack hut selling delicious currywest and fries. The place for the night took some googling but I finally located a campsite 30 minutes up the road that would do nicely. The campsite turned out to be a fairground, so I moved on. I pulled up outside a bar close by and asked some locals. "There is one just a kilometre up the road" a guy said, I thanked him and rode on and Hey Presto! he was right. Helmstedt was a perfect spot in the back grounds of an empty run-down hotel costing €10.50 and was well worth it. The camping was on nice level ground next to a forest. I had a couple of Weiss beers in the sun, read my Guy Martin book, then called it a night.

Helmstedt Campsite - Germany

Tuesday 15/05/2018

It was a quiet spot and I slept pretty well despite the occasional "is there an axe killer looming in the woods" thought. I had found my sleeping mat uncomfortable at the Sunart Rally, but the secret is not to over inflate it. Last night it proved to be very comfortable. I took it easy in the morning and made some coffee. "Must be more Raymond" I thought to myself. Raymond - who I travelled with on the Argentina to Alaska trip - was great at slowing things down. Sometimes drove me off my nut mind you but I need to slow down.

It was good to have a sunny, dry morning to pack up in and soon I was on my way. I stopped off at a McDonalds for a German breakfast meal. "What no hash brown" I murmured. I ordered an orange juice to add some fruit to my diet. It was then just a case of riding east towards Poland. The Berlin ring was busy but thankfully my side kept moving. I noticed a road sign for

Alexanderplatz where Amber and I had stayed during a Berlin break a few years back. It had been a good weekend. I stopped to fuel up a couple of times and had lunch at a service station. It was there I got chatting to some Harley riders from Belgium who were heading to a rally - I later caught up with a Dutch couple doing the same. I checked the location and as it was in the right general direction, I decided I would go too.

I cheered as I entered Poland, Boris had earned a new flag! I pulled over at the first service station to exchange some cash. I had only discovered last night that Poland is not using the Euro. I headed on past Poznan then turned north for Bydgoszcz. Initially it was a brand-new two-lane highway but soon it turned into a regular A road. So far Poland was looking as I expected. An older style of place undergoing modernisation is how I would describe it.

I was feeling good with only 35 kilometres to go when the traffic came to a halt. After a bit, everyone started turning around. Not great I thought. There were two DPD delivery vans in front of me, so I decided to follow them. First up a rough road over railway tracks and then onto a deep sand track. My worst nightmare! Something to avoid in Mongolia but this was Poland. It was downhill and there was no turning back. The cool text-book way to deal with deep sand is to power through it. The very uncool way (my chosen option) is to get into the gutter and have your legs flap and scream in terror as the front wheel wallows.

Thankfully, I made it down the hill and it became a mixture of packed sand and gravel, so I powered my way through that. Still, I had lost the DPD vans and had no idea if I was going in the right direction. I found out I wasn't as I reached a dead end. I remembered what looked like a junction a bit further back, so I turned around and headed for that. A car came along and took that turn too so I felt it must be right. Another flappy foot section through more deep sand and I was in a dense forest but with a firmer track. There were a couple of options at one point, but I just went with my gut and Hey Presto! I popped out beyond the road closure. Was it stressful? Yes!

I was so glad to be on tarmac, normal service had resumed. I had been messing with google maps and had my phone connected via my earplugs. Out of the blue at full volume "Loch Lomond" by

Runrig started playing. I nearly jumped out of my skin. When I realised what it was, I smiled and started singing along.

Bydgoszcz was a decent sized town, thankfully Google maps did its job and got me to the gates of the FH-DCE Super Rally. I was not sure what to do to start with but decided just to go and ask if I could stay the night. The guys ushered an English-speaking lady over and after hearing my story she said yes with a smile, although I would have to be gone by 2pm the next day. I rode in and onto one of the camping fields. A dour looking marshal rode up to me on a Road King telling me to stop. He was clearly not happy to see me but grudgingly accepted the fact I had been let in.

The rally site was massive but as it did not officially start until Wednesday, it was very quiet. I pitched up and wandered around to check the place out. "Hey Scotsman" rang out from the outdoor restaurant. It was the Belgian guys. One of them thrust a meal voucher into my hand and said "With compliments of us for your trip." I went to shake hands, but he did that cool hand grasp thing that I kind of missed. Still it wasn't as uncool as when at a Miami Dolphins game, I responded to an Americans fist bump by grabbing his fist. My children are still embarrassed by that one. A couple of Polish beers and it was time for me to hit the sack.

Wednesday 16/05/2018

It was exceptionally quiet for even a pre-rally overnight, although I wasn't complaining. I woke up early so had plenty of mulling time before the rally came alive. Last night I had pondered my next move, this morning I confirmed it. I would do a short 2-hour ride to Gdansk and have a leisurely day in what is described as one of Poland's prettiest cities and home to the Lech Walesa revolution. I booked myself into Hotel Bonum in the city centre which was reasonably priced and in a great location. That would leave me two days to do the 11-hour ride to get to my pre-border destination of Lucia.

The ride was dull and a little boring. It reminded me of Panama with both the terrain and the road construction. At one point I pulled into a service station to use an ATM. While standing there, an older Australian man came up and asked about my trip. He was an ex sidecar racer and was on his way via a European tour to the Bob McIntyre trophy at East Fortune in Scotland. We had a good chat.

I pulled back onto the highway. I forgot to mention the second half of the journey was on motorway. As soon as I flipped my helmet down a very bad version of "I belong to Glasgow" began playing loudly in my ears. That same action had brought on Loch Lomond yesterday. Now I could have whipped the earphone cable out, but it would have flapped about, so I decided to welly it to the next rest area. Five excruciating repeats later I had it off. Flipping down the helmet was now on the pre-ride check list.

I found the hotel easily and they directed me around the rear to park the bike. It was just like old times in South America, securing the tyres to the bike and putting a cover over it, I made several runs from the bike to the room with gear and finally was ready for that much awaited shower! It was a joy and I washed my dirty clothes in there with me. A fresh and clean version of me was ready to go walk the city. It really was pretty, especially on such a sunny day. I had a small platter lunch and a herring sandwich dinner. I had made the right decision to come here. I could have paid the money and stayed another day at the rally but the semi-grudged reception I got from the organisers put me off. The last straw was when I asked via a friendly Polish worker if I could buy a rally sticker and was met with a gruff no.

Time now for a real bed.

Thursday 17/05/2018

I awoke to what I thought was the sound of rain. "Oh no!" I thought but oh yes it was, as I peeked out the window. Rain is fine except for a few things; firstly, the packing of the bike is unpleasant and secondly, I discovered I cannot use the phone mount power and earphones with the rain cover on. That's important because I am going on a strange route and my out of date Garmin has proven its inadequacies. So, with all that in mind I decided I would take a longer route today. Rather than head straight east, I would go south east to Warsaw then north from there. My logic for this circa 2 hours add-on was that

Warsaw is well signposted and that the rain was due to clear by the afternoon. Was it a good idea? Probably not.

It was a wet start with a fair bit of traffic and a whole load of diversions. Poland is investing majorly in its road network. In fact, the roads I had been on the journey so far were all far superior to the pot holed UK ones. I finally emerged out of the rain and traffic diversions and had a clear run down to Warsaw. My only stops were for food and fuel as I turned north again. More road building, rain and diversions then once again I emerged into the sunshine. I wanted to get within 300 miles of my Latvia hotel which is the jumping off point for Russia, but since I had Polish currency to spend, I didn't want to cross the border. The perfect spot was Augustow near the Lithuanian border.

I stopped and fuelled up at the edge of town, had a good friendly conversation with a Ukrainian, then googled close-by hotels. I had noticed signs for the Hotel Wanazawan, so that tempted me in. At just over £30 it was a no brainer. The hotel was still under its final internal fix but the room, location and food were great and the parking was secure.

It had been a tough but good day. Tomorrow, Lithuania and Latvia.

Friday 18/05/2018

The sun shone through the curtains as I awoke, which is always a welcome bonus. I started my packing routine and whilst downstairs checked on the breakfast start time - 7am. Breakfast was average but good in terms of setting me up for a decent uninterrupted start to the days riding. I decided to divide my ride into three 100-mile stints with short breaks at each point. Google Maps was showing 7 hours, so I guess it wasn't going to be super highways. Although flat, Northern Poland had turned out to be prettier than I expected. Lithuania was similar but a bit poorer and Latvia had the same type of countryside but poorer still. I have to say it's impressive how much infrastructure/highway building that is going on in all three countries. Europe is going to be very connected.

I pulled up at a local roadside restaurant for lunch in Lithuania and noticed a Dutch plated Ducati Multi-Strada. I wondered if it could be the guy going on Alex's tour. I said "Hi" when I entered but he just nodded and didn't seem that interested, so I left it at that.

The rain came on in Latvia, adding to its poorer look but cleared an hour or so before my destination of Lucia. I was weary when I arrived and glad to see the hotel. It looked like what might have been a town hall. Quite grand in a way, at least on the outside. Inside was very Eastern European basic but perfectly fine. I did my unpacking, took a shower then wandered downstairs. There, standing in reception was the same Dutch guy I had spotted earlier. I had to ask, "Are you Dirk"?

"I am" he replied.

He told me that he had been to the border, but his Sat Nav had not revealed any hotels on the Russian side, so he had randomly picked this one. What are the chances of stopping at the same lunch spot then meeting in the same hotel?

I left him to it and took a wander around the square. I then headed down to the basement of the hotel for dinner. Just after I ordered, Dirk arrived and asked if he could join me. We had a pleasant conversation and agreed we would meet for breakfast the next morning and cross the border together. Back up in my room I tried out my Russian Garmin maps. The free download did nothing for me but after painstakingly typing in the Cyrillic version of my Moscow hotels address the eBay purchased version jumped into life. Result!

Saturday 19/05/2018

8am is a late breakfast for me but that was the start time. Before then I had Boris packed, watched half a movie and mulled around. Breakfast was great value at four euros for an omelette and bread.

Dirk had a modern Sat Nav which covers Russia through to Moscow, so he took the lead. It was a beautiful morning as we made the short ride to the Russian border. I noticed a small Roe deer running across the road in front of Dirk and a flock of birds flew above us. "They don't care about borders or politics" I thought to myself. We reached the Latvia exit point with only four cars in front of us. It was all very familiar from the last trip. Border equals exit point, no man's land and entry point.

I thought to myself "this might be quick." An hour and a half later when nothing had moved, I conceded it would not,

Just around then two heavily packed GS Adventures pulled up behind us. One German and one Austrian plate. Amazingly it was another two guys on the Alex's tour. As I anticipated, Wolfgang the German headed off to find out what was happening while we chatted to Joseph the Austrian. German's don't hang back in my experience. Wolfgang came back with no information and whispered under his breath about an unhelpful lady. These boys had seriously accessorised bikes and had done some impressive touring.

We were eventually called forward to the next stage of the process then, after another long wait, were waved on to the Russian entry. They ushered us into our own lane, gave us some forms then ignored us for an hour. All in, we had to visit three windows and the amount of paperwork the clerks filled in was mind blowing. Four and a half hours later Wolfgang and Joseph were off and soon after Dirk and I pulled out.

I did smile about the fact they arrived behind us but left before us.

Next up was fuel for Dirk and Insurance for me. The first petrol station delivered both but not before pre-paying for your fuel and another torturous paperwork filling session. Insurance cost £27 and lasted for 3 months. At long last we were on our way. The sat navs could not locate the hotel but thankfully I had read how far along the road it was so, I set my sights on 150 miles.

I took the lead setting a healthy but sensible pace. The road was in brilliant condition, mainly straight with forest on either side with little traffic. We made great progress and after a fuel stop, we finally reached mile 150 and pulled over at a small turn off. Unbelievably the hotel entrance was right across the road.

We drove down a dirt road and passed through automated security gates and were welcomed by a girl in traditional dress.

They acknowledged my booking and thankfully had a cabin for Dirk too. The place made me smile. It was like a log cabin holiday park that had not quite had the funds to be completed. The cabin was great for me and the dinner was much needed and appreciated as our lunch had been consumed by the border crossing. One border down and three to go.

Sunday 20/05/2018

We made a relaxed start as the weather forecast predicted rain in the morning but clearing up in the afternoon. We made good progress on mainly straight, well-maintained roads. As we neared Moscow the road turned into Motorway and traffic became denser. It had stayed dry for most of the way but it started to rain quite heavily at that point. Worst possible timing! I was following Dirk as his Sat Nav was more modern, but my Russian eBay version was tracking with him which bode well. After a few traffic hold-ups and a lot of concentration we entered Moscow, stopped for fuel then made our way to the hotel. I had been told horror stories about Russian drivers but to be honest it I thought the Polish drivers were worse.

There was a GS parked outside the hotel with a Scottish plate. We parked up beside it and checked in. The hotel was great, so it was a case of chilling for a few hours. Later, I noticed Josef and Wolfgang pulling up outside. As I passed reception, I met Alex the tour lead, Andree a Canadian lady and Graham Vavangas (the owner of the GS) who was English but lived in Aberdeen. We headed out to dinner where I met Mark, an American and Jacques, another Canadian. They all seemed very nice.

Dinner was at a Ukrainian buffet type place which was very touristy but good fun with lots of music, singing and laughter. The food was a mixture of good and bad but a great way of finding what might work. On the walk to and from the restaurant I was gobsmacked by how beautiful Moscow is.

Moscow - Russia

Monday 21/05/2018

Next morning was glorious and Alex had a walking tour arranged with Evgenia, a charming young unofficial guide. We walked for miles covering the Kremlin, KGB building and lots of other interesting spots. Moscow was also prepared and decked out for the forthcoming world cup. Stunning, friendly city is how I would sum Moscow up.

The highlight of my day was when both Andree and Wolfgang were found to be carrying knives (multi-tools) at the Kremlin security entrance. Evgenia turned around and said, "Do any more of you have knives with you". I was amazed by how calmly the security guys took it

We headed out - using the very impressively decorated underground - that evening to a local restaurant which was very nice. On the way back, we shared a bottle of Vodka in a bar close to the hotel. It was a nice way to end to the evening.

Tuesday 22/05/2018

Nobody fancied the planned long walking tour that day, so we elected to go with Evgenia on a short Moscow river boat trip. I think we were all just killing time as the road was calling. I managed to change money in a little secure cupboard within a supermarket, which was a relief. I enjoyed chilling in the hotel that afternoon.

The second tour guide Alex - to be known as "Alex II" - arrived on a well-used old Honda Africa Twin. He was a cool character who had travelled the world extensively on his beloved bike. I liked him.

Dinner was at a steak and burger place within walking distance from the hotel. It was great quality food and had a good lively atmosphere. I could have been in Glasgow, London or New York.

Wednesday 23/05/201

Group departure day.

We met up early as planned and set off on what was a sunny day. As we pulled out of the hotel it was like the opening scene of Wild Hogs with Marks legs flailing, Andrea over-revving the engine and Jacques looking decidedly unsteady. "This will be fun" I thought smiling to myself. To be fair this was their first run on hired bikes and it takes time to adjust. We followed Alex down to the street to a spot where he could take a good picture of us with the Kremlin in the background. The traffic was much quieter than I had expected although the ride out of town took forever, passing through some very unattractive suburbs.

Our first stop was for fuel. The "fuel included in the price" party all lined up behind Alex while Graham and I were left to do our own thing. In Russia you must pay first then fill-up. Thankfully Graham spoke a bit of Russian which made things easier.

We then stopped at an old church in Vladimir which was interesting. From there we left the highway and snaked through various villages in flat mainly wooded countryside. We visited a ruined mansion as suggested by Graham but I felt it was not worth the detour. Our bonding started when I told him to refrain from making suggestions with a smile. From there it was on to a very late lunch stop.

The entry into Nizhniy Novgorod, our destination, was ugly and busy but as soon as you hit the centre things got a lot more attractive. Our hotel stood high above the Volga river (Europe's longest) and our bikes were parked in an underground garage reminding me of Argentina. We arrived tired and overheated on what had been a long day. Wolfgang, Joseph and Jacques did their own thing that night which was a good sign as I knew I would want a break away from the crowd sometimes too. For the rest of us, dinner involved a mosquito infested walk, so I was glad to get back to the hotel and get tucked up in bed.

Thursday 24/05/2018

I realised after yesterday's ride that this was no holiday. It was quite a punishing schedule each day. This morning we headed out of the busy city and soon hit the back roads again towards Kazan. The weather was still bright but a more comfortable temperature.

The further away from Moscow the better looking the countryside got. The roads were very variable from deep pot holes to smooth tarmac. The team had done a bit of forming and storming and were now reaching the norming stage, although there would always be some discussions. We had an established position, with me sitting behind Dirk and Graham behind me. That worked well. The least predictable was Josef who was like an Austrian Motorcycle herder, zooming back and forward directing traffic. All in our best interests of course.

Lunch was special for me at least because it was a very local place in the bottom of one of the Soviet era house complexes. The food was great including sausages, vegetable soup and custard pastries. The people were reacting as though we had just come from outer space. I love seeing the curiosity in people's faces.

As the day progressed the weather deteriorated so we stopped off at a bus stop to let those who needed to, put on their rain gear. Further on Andree took a couple of tumbles in a petrol station as she lost her footing. The bike was just a little too tall for her.

Our destination Kazan is predominantly a Muslim city and I could hear the prayers being sung as we headed towards the hotel. It was a nice hotel with parking available in a secure courtyard. I unpacked, got changed then had a beer with Wolfgang and Joseph as we awaited the others.

We walked to the modern main street and the place was buzzing. The kids were all dressed up and there were bands playing, celebrating high school graduation. Our destination was the impressive white Kazan Kremlin. I was always under the impression that the only Kremlin was in Moscow, but Kremlin is the Russian word for castle - of which there are many. On the way one of the guys asked Alex II about the origins of a statue? I loved his reply "I am a motorcycle guide, not a historian".

I decided to wander back on my own ahead of the others. As I made my way I bumped into Jacques. We started to walk towards a pizza place when we spotted Alex waving at us. Our plans for a low-key pizza were thwarted. Dinner was Alex's choice of local cuisine which included bland horse meat and some delicious stuffed Nan type bread but no pizza.

Friday 25/05/2018

The schedule said a short off-road section was included today so we were all wondering what that entailed. The ride out of Kazan was busy but manageable and again the weather, roads and countryside were all great. I was settling into a rhythm. The off-road section turned out to be tightly packed sandy gravel so no issues at all. It was Dirk's first gravel experience, so he took his time but did great.

I noticed Jacques and Graham had flasks with them and had a cuppa at fuel stops. They filled them up at breakfast each day before heading off. It was a great idea.

After an event free ride, we arrived at our Izhevsk hotel in good time. It was a gigantic log cabin and we were greeted with a local vodka served by ladies in traditional dress. Dinner was taken in the hotel and I headed off for an early night while some went for a traditional sauna.

Left to Right – Myself, Mark, Jacques, Josef, Russian Lady, Wolfgang, Andre, Graham, Dirk and Alex II Izhevsk - Russia

Saturday 26/05/2018

Today we faced a four-hundred-mile ride and I was feeling refreshed and ready for it. Big Mark succumbed to a bad camber as we headed out of the hotel car park and clattered to the ground. Thankfully he was fine. Getting out of the city was quieter than I expected which was a bonus. It was sunny but quite cool as we headed out of town. The ride was through the gentle rolling Ural hills which was scenic and had good quality roads, with one exception. Alex II took a wrong turn and we ended up on 40 kilometres of gravel. Although I don't enjoy it, I was pleased to do it as it helped me prepare for Mongolia. I was mainly reasonably comfortable, other than when Dirk hit a sandy section throwing up dust that blinded me. Hitting sand blind is not fun so it was a case of keeping the power on and waiting for it to clear. Lesson of that day was, stay further back.

Just before our destination of Yekaterinburg, we made a stop at the Europe – Asia Oblique. Everyone was on high spirits having ridden their motorcycles to Asia. From there it was a short ride into town and the hotel. I stayed out of the company that night and had a beer and a burger in the bar. Andree had something in her eye and headed off to see a doctor with Alex in support. That young man works hard for his money. She was well treated and felt better after some grit was removed.

Sunday 27/05/2018

Bliss! A rest day at last! Nothing better after some hard riding days filled with company than to chillax on my own. A city tour had been arranged for the afternoon, but I would avoid it as I needed some me-time. I took a walk around the city in the morning and found nothing much of interest but it was good to stretch the legs. In the afternoon I headed through a nice park which was really peaceful on that pleasant sunny Sunday. I could hear church services going on in the background which added to the atmosphere. I had a look at the church which was built on the site where the gruesome murder of the last Tsar family "the Romanov's" took place. It was a horrible story of a botched murder of a family of men, woman and children. I don't know whether they were a good or bad family, but it was ugly.

In the late afternoon I arranged to meet up with Alex II to discuss Mongolia as he had ridden it. He arrived in his usual cool manner smoking a small thin cigar. Firstly, he checked if I had the free maps for my Garmin which I confirmed I did. We then studied the paper map. He recommended I take the southern route. He gave a couple of tips on Ger camps and warned me about the corrugation on the gravel roads. I was aware of how horrible that was from my trip in Argentina.

I had arranged a FaceTime call that evening with my parents while Amber visited them. My mother looked very frail and gaunt. Feelings of guilt stayed with me for a while. Old age is not something I am looking forward to.

I went out to dinner that night to a cool German themed restaurant with Alex II and a few others. Alex stayed back as he was trying to shake off a fever that had apparently been plaguing him for a few days.

Monday 28/05/2018

Another exciting milestone lay ahead today. We were bound for Siberia and its unofficial western capital of Tyumen. Siberia is just one of those places that conjures up so many images in my mind. Mainly cold, wild, remote and imprisonment. On the way out of town we stopped off at the site where the Romanov's bodies had been mutilated and buried. It had now been turned into a monastery with a church built for each member of the family. It was a serine place in the middle of a beautiful forest.

Our next stop was in the town of Irbit where they manufacture the Ural sidecar outfit. Firstly, we visited a private museum where I had a go at riding or is it driving a sidecar which was fun. After that we visited the factory itself. It was the most run-down factory I have ever encountered with only a few buildings used in what had been a massive complex. Even the car park was a disgrace. Ural is an iconic brand, and this is an opportunity waiting to be grasped. Just look at the success of Royal Enfield as an example.

We finally arrived in Tyuman which was a clean modern city and we ate out at another German themed restaurant. Alex II now had the fever.

Tuesday 29/05/2018

This was the beginning of what was described as two high mileage highway days. For the first time we split as a group with the Austrian- German team deciding to leave later. The rest of us left at 6am to avoid city traffic and trucks.

It was just under 400 miles and the weather was sunny but cold. As soon as we left town, I could see swampland on either side of the highway making me think how impassable this country would have been in the past. Progress was good although the fuel stops were a bit close to the bone. By the time we did the first one I had seven miles left in my tank. Lunch was at a truck stop which was cheap and wholesome. I caught my first sight of a Russian pit toilet in the car park. It was pretty disgusting.

The roads deteriorated as we approached the city of Omsk, which is apparently rich but corrupt. It was unattractive on the way in and remained that way for me. Dinner that night was excellent in a restaurant overlooking the Irtysh river.

Wednesday 30/05/2018

I felt a bit down as I awoke for marathon day number two. I had soreness on my lip which usually indicates stress or it may have been the constant exposure to the weather. I had been having bad dreams for the last few nights which didn't help. The road was long and mainly straight, and I passed the time singing to myself.

We had some drama at our fuel stop when Dirk declared he had lost his passport. He franticly searched his luggage with a look of worry on his face. Thankfully he found it in a pocket and calm was restored.

The ride had started out dry but a hundred or so miles from Novosibirsk we could see a big storm ahead. Such was the flat vastness of the area you could see many different weather systems. It had been relatively cold all the way and we were now riding in torrential rain with lightning strikes all around us. Thankfully it didn't take too long before we emerged from the storm and in a flash the temperature rose from 12 to 20 degrees.

It was extreme, bizarre and something I had never experienced before.

Novosibirsk was massive and very busy as we made our way into the city centre. The hotel was large and modern and, as it was nearly 8pm already, I was glad to hear we were eating in the onsite restaurant. A few vodkas were consumed as we had a rest day tomorrow.

Thursday 31/05/2019

After a more leisurely start than normal, Graham and I rode a few kilometres to the BMW dealer. Like most I experienced in South America it was a car dealership with a motorcycle corner. The friendly staff served us coffee while we waited for the mechanic. He arrived just after 10am and immediately asked to see the bikes. He was a likeable, tattooed guy in his early thirties and thankfully he knew some basic English. I explained I needed an oil and filter change, my tyres swapped over and the application of a tyre sealant that I had carried with me from the UK. He seemed fine with that.

The rain came on heavy and continued through the day. We discussed whether the walking tour was a good idea but, in the end, agreed to go. It started with a hair-raising taxi ride which lasted about an hour to an open-air train museum. Now on a nice day that would be good but we all felt miserable in the pouring rain. I must say the trains were huge and impressive and we got some respite from the rain by exploring the carriages. The hospital and prison carriage were the best. We all agreed to call it a day early and headed back to the hotel.

Graham received a message from the mechanic that he needed to change my rear brake pads. I was surprised as I had new ones fitted before leaving but told him to go-ahead regardless. An hour or so later Graham and I caught a cab to go pick up the bikes. They looked great having been washed. The mechanic handed me back the unused bottle of Tyre Seal saying he did not want to put anything in my tyres that might disturb the balance. To be fair I had been a bit unsure about it myself.

Thankfully, by then it was sunny and the roads were drying out. It was a slow run back due to traffic and I opted for quiet night eating in the hotel restaurant. Just after I sat down Jacques arrived and asked me if he could join me. He had picked up a fever from the two Alex's which worried me a bit, but I could hardly say no. I liked Jacques and had a nice time chatting away. Sadly, he had decided to take the train from that point on and ship the bike. I think it was a combination of his illness and the fast pace that had led him to that decision.

Friday 01/06/20

And then there was one.

I had originally planned to leave around 10am letting the others head off at 9am, but as usual I was up early. I decided I would go see the others off and leave just after. I had mixed feelings about it. They were a good bunch and I would miss the company, but I looked forward with some fear and trepidation to being solo again. We all shook hands and said our goodbyes and I filmed them as they headed off into the sunrise.

The ride out of the city was painless after negotiating around a car accident. I had passed two accidents on the trip, both in Novosibirsk. It took quite a while to leave the suburbs behind but eventually I was out and surprisingly on a dual carriageway. After some time, I exited onto an A road taking a more southerly route towards the Russian Atal Republic region. The land became drier (less marshlands) with small undulating hills.

It was a warm day, so I pulled over to a petrol station to strip off my fleece and change my gloves. As I emerged from the petrol station there were road works which I manoeuvred around as best as I could to get back onto the main road. As soon as I did, I was pulled over by a cop. I stepped off the bike removed my helmet and smiled. "Documents" he said. I tried to explain I was from Scotland, but he was struggling to understand so I tried the bagpipes mimic then whisky. He suddenly smiled and said "William Wallace". I shouted "freedom" and we both laughed. He pointed to a solid white line that I had crossed then to his eyes as a "watch out" warning. We shook hands and I was indeed free.

The countryside improved as I moved forward with rivers and hills all around. I eventually rolled into Gorno-Altaysk and with the assistance of Garmin Co-ordinates found my out of the way hotel easily. When I say hotel, it was more like a house rental and there was no one at home. I called a number on a sign and within 5 minutes a mother and baby arrived to let me in and show me the facilities. Within 15 minutes she was gone, and it seemed I had the house to myself. I took a shower and enjoyed getting organised in this quiet place. I wandered into town and had a delicious burger from a Russian fast food joint.

I had contacted Kate, my Russian wing woman whose details Hutch's friend Kenny had provided. He knew her from past work experience. There had been conflicting stories concerning the weekend opening hours of the border and I had been trying to find out the facts - without success. She was brilliant and within a few hours she confirmed Saturday open 9am – 5pm and Sunday closed. Now I had a dilemma, do I make a mad dash tomorrow, or do I wait it out? I was tired anyway, so I decided to have an early night and start off early leaving my options open. My other worry of the evening was that while researching the border, I read in a blog that you must have an international drivers' licence to enter Mongolia. I had not seen that anywhere else and did not have one.

Around 10pm I was awoken by the noise of someone trying to unlock the door. Apparently, there were other guests and I had left the key in the door. I scrambled around frantically in the dark and opened the door to a handsome young couple in my underpants. Not a good end to the evening for them!

Saturday 02/06/2018

Since I was in bed by 8pm, I was awake just after 4am so I lay around for an hour to let the sun come up. I then quietly packed up Boris avoiding awakening last night's barking dog next door. I noticed that I had left my usb charger, that I had had fitted to Boris, live overnight. Had it drained the battery? I opened the gates pressed the starter button and thankfully he fired up and I was off.

I later discovered that I had left my washing hanging on a clothes line. That was 20% of my clothes gone, including my brand new Rumototravel T-Shirt.

The roads and countryside got even better as I left town. It was a novelty to be on twisty roads again and the scenery reminded me of Colorado. It was a long ride sprinkled with a few picture taking stops as I headed south. Snow-capped mountains appeared in the horizon and the surrounding countryside turned into high plains desert like New Mexico. These were the best roads and scenery of the trip so far.

Great roads with stunning scenery in the Altai region of Russia

I eventually arrived at Kosh Agach and deliberately rode past my hotel which was on the northern edge of town. My plan was to ride to the border and take a look. As I rode on, I said to myself "I have time. If I go to the border now there is only 4 hours to get through. What if I am refused entry due to the International Drivers Licence. Would I have time to re-enter Russia? I am also throwing away a non-cancellable booking." I stopped, did a U-turn and headed to the hotel.

The check-in experience was interesting as there was only one guy shrugging his shoulders. I managed to get a phone number from him and called a woman who in turn had another English-speaking woman call me back. I was given a key to a nice dual aspect room which was boiling hot. The hotel was new but not quite functional yet, as I discovered the air con and Wi-Fi did not work. It was also too far out of town to walk; it might be a long two days. The English-speaking woman got the guy to drive me to the only restaurant, but I decided to buy some bits and pieces from the supermarket and have a quiet night in.

Sunday 03/06/2018

I had wondered how Sunday would go with no real town or internet, but it turned out fine. One of the highlights was an invitation by two Russian ladies - accompanying a young Canadian on a Russian Altai tour - to join them for breakfast. Freshly made pancakes with jam and tea was much better than the dry bread and cheese I had planned. They told me about their tour company and how one of them was married to a Dutchman who worked in Eindhoven, as had I for 4 years. They gave me some insight into the local area, such as the existence of snow leopards which surprised me. They also told me a great story of how a visiting native American found they had similarities in the language of the more remote settlements. This points back to the migration of people east when there was a land bridge between Asia and America. They invited me to go north with them to some sites which I politely declined. I asked one of the ladies to ask the guy if I could move to the smaller but shaded room for that night. He was surprised but was happy for me to do so.

One good thing about the hotel was they had a secure garage for the bike overnight so I asked the guy to open it up. I rode Boris to a shaded area in front of the hotel and performed a nuts and bolts check. I had to tie-wrap up a bit of headlight cabling but other than that it was good. While I was working on the bike another adventure biker suddenly appeared. I think his name was

Alfredo and he was probably in his mid to late thirties. He was a friendly Spanish guy riding around the world on a nice Honda 500x with soft luggage. We chatted for a while and I explained that the border was shut. He asked about the price of this hotel and when I told him I could tell it was a bit too expensive. He told me he would go and have a look around town and decide later.

I rode into town and visited the little supermarket again for some more cheese and fresh bread then returned to the hotel and chilled watching some downloaded movies. My supper of bread, cheese, cold sausage and warm Heineken was one not to cherish.

It had been a relaxing Sunday.

Monday 04/06/2018

I decided I would get to the border just before opening to give me plenty of time to get across or not. I did think about the not and my only choice would be a two day backtrack then head to Ulan-Ude. That would be manageable but not desirable and maybe a little humiliating. No Russian ladies to make breakfast this morning so it was dry bread and cheese served with Nescafé.

The ride to the border seemed to take a little longer than I expected but maybe it was just anxiety playing with my head. I arrived before 9am as planned and there were around seven cars in front of me. After a while I was waved to the front and let through.

The next security guys ushered me to an area with outdoor tables for bag checks. "Empty your luggage onto the tables" a gruff guy said. "Do you have pills"? I did as he said and handed over my First Aid bag containing my pills. He quickly spotted a non-prescription strong pain killer which included codeine. He looked almost satisfied that he had something on me. He asked me if they were prescribed and I responded "no," then he spoke to someone on his radio. Another, more officious guy arrived, looked at the pills asked for my passport and ordered me to wait there. At this point I wasn't too worried. Surely, I can't be in bother with non-prescription pills from Boots Pharmacy.

I waited around for about an hour and was wondering if they had forgotten about me. I decided to stay calm and do nothing. Eventually, the more officious guy ordered the officious guy to get me to load my bike and take it behind the office building next to the sniffer dog kennels. This was now getting a little bit worrying. Three officers and two local guys - who looked as if they had been pulled from the street - came around and I was photographed with them holding the pills next to the bike and First Aid kit. Now I was really worried; who are these guys, is this a set-up? Again, I kept calm and went with the flow. I had been there two hours by that point. They then took me into the office block and up to the second floor. As we walked along the corridor, I scanned for cell doors. Thankfully it was just an office he showed me into. Again, I was left for a bit then a third officious guy returned with an English-speaking female guard. She was friendly and explained that although her English was poor, she was to be my interpreter. He took down all my details including name, address, date of birth, nationality, marital status etc. I had to detail my route through Russia to-date. I was then read what sounded like my rights over article 20, he then asked me about where and when I purchased the pills and their intended use. This was scary as there was no indication what was coming next. Eventually after 4 hours they had me sign some forms and I was told I could go.

It was with great relief that I mounted the bike and headed for the Mongolian check point. The Russian exit was supposed to be the easy bit. There was maybe five kilometres of no-man's land before I reached the first Mongolian check point manned by one guard. He took Boris's licence plate number and radioed ahead. Beyond the gate was a gravel road leading into the distance. After a few minutes he opened the gate and I was through. There were a number of cars ahead of me but a money change guy waved me forward. I was pleased to see Antonio parked there too. He greeted me and apologised for not coming back to my hotel last night. I told him it wasn't a problem. It turned out that Antonio was Gregorio and he was forty-two.

The next bit was pandemonium as everybody jostled to get served at the window. While we were waiting, a retired German couple in a monster truck arrived. We all eventually got to the next stage which was passport control, police, then customs. There was no bag check and even more importantly there was no ask for an International driver's licence. I was good to go. Predictably the Germans arrived after us and left before us. How do they do it?

I waited for Gregorio and we both headed down the road. Not for long though, as within twenty meters we were pulled over by a lady cop. She was friendly and took us to a room where they processed road tax and insurance for a sum of about ten pounds then sent us on our way. I mentioned to Gregorio that I had read this road to Altai was the dodgiest, with people pretending they had broken down and robbing you. We were about a kilometre down the gravel road when a guy on a small motorcycle tried to pull us over. We ignored him, and he harassed us like an annoying wasp for half an hour or so but finally gave up. Gregorio had told me he rode very slow and asked me to move on if I wanted. I also ride cautiously on gravel but did lose him after a while. I tried to wait a couple of times but got harassed by the motorcycle wasp, so I moved on. I eventually hit good tarmac and zoomed towards town. Mongolia looked like the southern Russian Altai, which was wild and wonderful. I saw what looked like a golden eagle fly over my head. "This is Mongolia," I said to myself proudly.

There was a short hill pass where the road became gravel again, which made me wonder if I was on the right route. This would not be the last time I wondered that. The tarmac reappeared and before long I was rolling into Ulgii. Not long after entering, a guy in a Mongolian Tours Prius shouted over to me. "If you want good accommodation, please follow me." Firstly, I was surprised to see a Prius, then I checked with my gut and thought "this should be ok," I followed him for a couple of kilometres and we bumped down off the Main Street and into a courtyard with a house and a few Gers. He showed me a very basic room in the house or a very grubby looking Yurt. I agreed to the room in the house with dinner and breakfast for €20. He was very pushy which was annoying me – mostly around money exchange etc. Suddenly there was a panic and he ordered his daughter and I into his car. I asked his English-speaking daughter what the score was and she explained they wanted me to lure another tourist in. I told them no. When they left, I decided I had had enough and rode off again. I passed them coming back and I just waved at them.

I spotted Gregorio behind me and he explained they had captured him. After telling them to back off, we had a discussion and decided to go with it. To be honest I'm glad I did. They ran us to the supermarket and got us a €10 unlimited data Sim card, so it was a good start. They transformed the Yurt into a great space for Gregorio, so he was happy too. We both took time to catch up on life via Wi-Fi before our dinner was served in the Ger. There were a few Russian tourists eating dinner in the house but with vodka bottles on display, they looked like they were ready for a session. The owner also told us three Russian bikers were staying and sure enough we heard them arrive later.

Dinner was dough covered, poor quality meat and sweet bread with tea. I can't say enjoyed it but it was my first hot meal since the pancakes. I bid Gregorio good night around ten and headed to bed. Thankfully, the Russians had gone from the house by then so it was nice and quiet.

Dinner in a Yurt with Gregorio – Ulgii, *Mongolia*

Tuesday 05/06/18

I was awake packed and had a breakfast of eggs and bread before Gregorio emerged from his Ger. I asked him if he wanted to ride together and he told me just to go ahead. We were connected by WhatsApp by then and would meet up further down the road. I guess I had mixed feelings. I loved the freedom but would have liked a wingman for this first proper gravel section.

I had double checked a couple of times which road it was out if town, as my Sat Nav was not helping. I saw a sign for Khovd which was reassuring. The problem with Mongolia and many other countries is there are multiple places with the same name and not always that far apart. I think that was what was confusing my Sat Nav. I came to a barrier just out of town which mysteriously rose up and I was on the road. It was a glorious day and I was in awe of the wildness of the countryside. There were very few signs of people and now and again I would pass horses and cattle wandering free. I passed a beautiful blue lake with a few settlements dotted along its edge.

I was aware the tarmac would only last for a bit and before I knew it, I was approaching trouble. The trouble was not gravel but the fact they were extending the tarmac road where the gravel was, so I was forced onto a sandy track with some gravel at times which was sometimes even hard to follow. Mongolians always create their own parallel routes. I had no sand experience other than Poland and as Boris weighs half a ton, this was not good. I dropped him soon after I started but thankfully a guy with his young son helped me pick him up. I moved forward as best I could praying it would not last long, but last long it did.

I zig zagged following this route for kilometre after kilometre getting warmer and more concerned that I was not on the right route. At one time I followed a guy on a small motorcycle which helped determine the route. Further on, I found myself away from the highway works and on a single-track path rather than a road. Clearly this was not right but I could see a road ahead on my Sat Nav, so I stuck with it. I manoeuvred through some bumpy ground and a short river crossing and thankfully I came back to the highway. I made the mistake of showing a local a map and he pointed to a spot a lot further South than I should be. I was getting really concerned but I was aware locals might never even have seen a map, so I moved forward. This was taking hours; I was hot and I was running out of water. Fuel was beginning to worry me too.

I rode on for a bit and thought I must have passed Khovd by now so waved down some guys in a minivan. They were locals and they all poured over my map and pointed south of where I should be, then motioned down the road saying "China." My heart sank and as I pondered, I saw some big motorcycles coming towards us. It was the three Russians, so I frantically waved them down. "Is this the way to Khovd?" I asked. The first guy replied "Yes, it is about 50 Kilometres further on and you should be on tarmac soon." I thanked them and rode with them for a while. Riding with them was way above my normal pace but I was confident because I was not alone. At times we bumped onto the highway under construction but that often resulted in a U-turn with the way forward being blocked off.

At one point the lead rider and I got away from the other two so he stopped and politely told me I could move on as he would wait for his friends. In other words, "bugger off!" I had hoped to ride with them to town but at least I knew they were behind me.

I came to another section which took me far from the highway. There was some kind of industrial operation, so I pulled up to ask for help. Two guys were just getting into a Land Cruiser and I was delighted when one spoke English. I asked him if the town was nearby and he said it was about twenty kilometres away. I told him I was lost and asked for directions. He told me he needed to go to his camp first but after that he would send me on the right road. So off he went with me following further and further into the tundra. I knew in my heart that these roads were getting too sandy and that I could not keep up, but desperation made me try. Before long Boris' wheels dug in and I was thrown off quite hard with the Land Cruiser disappearing into the distance. I waved but they were gone.

I had no other choice than try and get moving again. I stripped off the panniers and tyres and tried to heave Boris up but I could not get him fully upright. I then used my feet to dig out a ditch under the tyres, so he would effectively slide in. That worked then and I found myself holding him on the wrong side for mounting. I swung my left leg over being careful with my balance, which succeeded. I then started the engine and got him to a stable place.

I was thirsty, so I reached in the pannier for my coffee mug which contained the last of my water. Unfortunately, it was leaking so I had to be content with a sip. While I was repacking, the Land Cruiser reappeared and the guys apologised for leaving me. I was relieved to see them.

One of many falls – South Western Mongolia

I explained the road was too sandy. He said "follow me," moving straight off the road into the Tundra at a slower but still reasonable pace. I cringed as I entered the Tundra as I had no idea what the surface would be like. To my great relief it was fairly firm. I screamed with delight as I chased him like a Comanche pursuing a Stagecoach across the desert. There was one sandy part, but it was short and manageable. After about five kilometres we were back at the highway and he bumped onto it. "Could this be it?" I said to myself "a road at last!" Unfortunately, that was not the case as we bumped back off before a bridge under construction. He stopped and asked me where I was from. I told him I was from Scotland and he told me he was Mongolian, and the older guy was Chinese. He told me to just follow the track and I would be in town soon. I thanked them both and moved on.

The track came to a junction shortly thereafter, the obvious choice seemed right, so I took it. The road was atrocious but within a few kilometres I could see what looked like a town in the distance. As I neared the town the road got even worse, but I knew the end was in sight. First priority was to get petrol which was not straight forward due to the construction, but eventually I found a way. I asked the guy at the pump for water, but he shook his head. I asked him if there was a hotel and he smiled and pointed into town. It was around 7pm now and I was exhausted. I stopped at the first building with a hotel sign and went in. At first the receptionist indicated there were no rooms then backtracked and said she had one luxury at around €40. I grabbed it straight away and put the bike around the back in a compound. As I entered the hotel a guy approached me offering help, including putting my bike in a truck as the roads were very bad. I took his card but told him I did not need any help. I was then approached by a lady in reception trying to sell me local goods. It was bad timing, all I needed was water, food and rest in that order, so I politely declined. The luxury room was basic but had a lounge and bedroom. Anything with a bed and working shower was good enough for me. I went to the restaurant and ate bad salad and soup served by a surly young woman. As I headed for bed a guy asked me where the rest of the riders were. It turned out he thought I was part of the BMW GS Rally that was happening in Mongolia that same week. It had been a hell of a day.

Wednesday 06/06/2018

I got up before the hotel staff and got organised for the day. I took a walk into town and was delighted after a third attempt to get some cash from an ATM. I visited a supermarket and bought some supplies - including four large bottles of water and a fruit/nut mix. According to my map the first half of the road to Altai would be tarmac with the second half being gravel. I just hoped it actually would be gravel. I negotiated the roadworks to get out of town and within a couple of kilometres I was on much welcomed smooth tarmac.

It was another beautiful day and I rode at a sedate pace taking in the glorious scenery. I pulled over twice to take photos of a pack of camels and a herd of horses. It was relaxing and stress-free riding. Tension only started to set in as I approached the area where the tarmac allegedly ran out, I had fuel and loads of water, so I should be fine. Right in that tarmac ending area the road surface changed and I thought this is a newer section of road. Surely this is not going to last all the way to Altai but last it did.

I felt as if the gods were giving me break after yesterday as I rolled into Altai around 3pm. I noticed a hotel with a restaurant at the edge of town, but I passed it and had a little look around. It was a small place but had all I required with banks, small supermarkets and petrol stations. I went back to the hotel and got a good room for a good price. As I chilled around the hotel, I noticed a sign that I thought said Karaoke. I went into Google translate and sure enough it was. Turns out this is a big deal in Mongolia. Later that night the music and screeching voices echoed up to my room.

Thursday 07/06/2018

This day would be interesting as it contained the last alleged gravel section of the trip. I had already checked with the receptionist who confirmed there was 200 kilometres still unpaved of the 391 kilometres to Bayankhongor where the tarmac restarted. I had fuel, water and I knew there were three petrol stations in between. Maybe I could make it in a day if the gravel was good.

As I rode the first section, I was thinking about camping options, I was keen to camp but after Tuesday my biggest fear was getting Boris stuck somewhere in the sand away from the road. Maybe I should wait until I am further north away from the desert, I thought to myself. Another cracking day, more cracking views and all was good as I passed the village of Delger. I knew the tarmac would end soon and sure enough I could see a gravel road looming ahead. The transformation point was worn and very steep, so I took one of the many side paths around it and parked up. I checked all my straps for tension, let some air out my tyres, duct taped my Sat Nav to keep it in places and set off. It was very rough in comparison with the likes of Ruta 40 in Argentina. Poor old Boris was getting well shaken up, but it was manageable - until the inevitable occurred. Yes, they are building a highway and I was routed off the main road again only this time I was in the Gobi Desert, so it was even worse than Tuesday's experience.

It didn't take long for the first fall to happen which left Boris at quite a bad angle. I had envisioned as the major southern route that traffic would at least be regular, but not at all. With the many ad-hoc routes on offer, even if there was traffic, they may not be on this track. It was off with the spare tyres and luggage and commence lifting. With this one I could not get him fully upright, so I used a tyre as a leverage point. After more ditch digging, I finally got him up. I knew I had no chance of reaching Bayankhongor so I now set my site on Buutsagaan which was about a third of the way off-road. Track conditions were awful, and I dropped the bike six times before finally seeing the village in the distance. On each occasion I had to go through the same process, I was getting exhausted in the heat.

The last 10 kilometres seemed to take forever but I finally arrived. I asked some locals about fuel by pointing to my tank but they shook their head. One old guy drew an arrow and wrote 75 on the ground. This was a real worry as I had used much more fuel than normal due to being in first and second gear most of the time. I looked around the village and stopped and asked another guy who seemed to be saying 200 metres. His mate was in a truck and I asked if I could follow him and sure enough just around the corner was a petrol station. It was such a relief and I could not thank him enough.

It was getting later now so my next move was to get out of the village and find a camping spot. As I said. it was not an easy task because you needed to be away from all of the informal tracks as you could be run over. You should not be visible from the road and the ground needed to be hard enough to ride on. Finally, you need to be able to find your way back to the road. I was thinking about all of this when I saw two big bikes coming towards me. It was two Russian lads on a V-Storm and Caviga. They were from Vladivostok and were heading on the same route that I had just come from, so we exchanged info. They told me that the road I was on was great compared to what was in front of me. They said there was 177 kilometres of hell on earth from about 20 kilometres further up the road. I almost smiled at the irony of it all, I had hoped for better conditions, not worse. They also told me there was a hostel about 14 kilometres up the road and said I should stay there. I told them what lay ahead for them and they were delighted to hear there was fuel just over the hill. The V-Storm guy put his name and number in my phone and asked me to call him when I reached Vladivostok.

We parted ways and I soldiered on hoping for the hostel to appear. I had another hard fall but thankfully a young man in a passing car helped me heave Boris up, luggage and all. It was getting dark now and I had done well more than 14 kilometres, I had to make camp. I had noticed the ground is harder at the summits of the undulating desert so at the next summit I turned left off the road and rode for about a kilometre over very stony ground. I passed a track on the way which would help re-orient me on my return. As soon as I picked a spot, I swung Boris around and pointed him to where I had come from so I would know which direction I needed to head in the morning. I would probably not be out of sight of traffic, but it was dark now anyway and I was completely exhausted.

I pitched the tent using my head torch. I kept scanning the black horizon wondering if anyone would come. I felt a very vulnerable sitting there in the dark. I had hoped for a sea of stars but it was cloudy and threatened rain. I unpacked my stove and made a dry pack meal of pasta which I had carried from home. It was delicious, maybe helped by my stress and hunger. I crawled into the tent exhausted and had a right good deep desert sleep. What a day!

Forced camp on rocky ground – The Gobi Desert - Mongolia

Friday 08/06/2018

I had two targets this morning I thought to myself. The first one would be another village with fuel called Bumbuger (great name) which was two thirds of the way, then hopefully I could do the last third and reach Bayankhongor and tarmac. I was up around 6am and ready to go. I found the road fairly easily and edged forward. My new mantra was "keep moving forward, stay in the tracks, power where needed but take it easy." I kept repeating this as I edged forward. To be honest I think the weight of a full fuel tank was helping keep the front steady. I eventually came to the settlement which I presumed contained the hostel. I stopped and bought some water and - after a lot of sign language - had some soup and tea in a local café. The cooks husband came in later and we all laughed as he tried on my jacket and helmet. He was astounded by the weight and the armour.

I was now aware this was the part the boys said got worse and for about the next 5 kilometres they were right, with me going down once. Between there and Bumbuger it was certainly no worse than I had experienced. The local Bumbuger cops led me to the supermarket and petrol station where I filled up. I pulled over by a ruined building and rested in the shade. Final third to go.

Now the Russian boys would be in for a shock because the final third was on much better road which was a great relief and I had no more offs. It was true the tracks were less distinct, but the ground was firmer. The hardest bit was the final 20 kilometres where you can see the town in the valley, but the construction trucks had decimated the tracks. I finally pulled into Bayankhongor about 7pm exhausted but relieved. I looked for a hotel and after passing a couple, chose one which I hoped would be ok. After paying I found that it was far from it. The bed was terrible, the sheets were torn, the door didn't lock and even worse the shower didn't work. I washed in the sink, bought some crisps and ice cream from a supermarket and went to bed.

Saturday 09/06/2018

The hotel from hell maintained its status with loud arguing going on throughout the night. I looked at my map with the curtains open, as there was a power cut and thought "screw it I am going to Ulaanbaatar." I was up and out by 6am, throwing the keys at the drunk receptionist on the couch on the way past. Thankfully, a petrol station with a generator was open and I filled up. It was such a relief to get out of town and ride tarmac again. I had a little wobbly moment when just after town I was diverted onto gravel but thankfully it was just some roadworks. Some people will be reading this and think I'm a woos off-road - they may be right! I know I should have been riding harder in the sand at times but being alone I did not want to increase the risk of injury. All I can say is that sand was very challenging for me.

Safely back on the tarmac, which was bad at times with serious pot-holes, but still tarmac. I made great progress only allowing myself to stop at 100-mile intervals on this 400-mile route. I passed through a reasonable sized town after about 90 miles and was amazed to find out that for the next three hundred it was only occasional settlements. That led to petrol stress but thankfully I did not run out. I had a lunch of bad soup and white sugary coffee - the opposite of what I enjoy.

With maybe 50 miles to go I came upon a modern looking stop with toilets, a coffee shop and a restaurant. As I pulled in, I noticed the three Russian bikers were parked up. I went in and had good coffee and bad cheese cake and booked a hotel in Ulaanbaatar. I then located the Russians and thanked them again for their help on Tuesday.

I rode the final stretch into Mongolia's only city. It was massive, with me riding through the suburbs for 14 miles before reaching my hotel in the centre. Every third car was a white Prius. What is it with Prius' in Mongolia? The hotel was heaven on earth with a great room, clean beds, Wi-Fi and in a great location. I located the nearest Irish Pub and went seeking a burger and chips, which it delivered. I have to say of all the remote and exotic places I have travelled, rural Mongolia has by far the worst food and rural Mexico has by far the best. I'd had visions of a big celebration night, but that clean and comfortable bed called me home.

Sunday 10/06/2018

A free day in Ulaanbaatar lay ahead of me as I awoke to the sound of rain. Amazingly both bad rain days had occurred on non-riding days so far. Breakfast was excellent with a guy on hand to cook eggs done your way. I asked the hotel if I could borrow a brolly which I could, and I was ready to head out. I had done a little research and decided to go visit Genghis Khan square. It was grand but there was no sign of the traders that were mentioned in the lonely planet description. After that I went sticker hunting which always takes some time. On my way I passed well-guarded entrances to the French and Turkish embassies. After visiting a string of souvenir shops, I finally found the perfect stickers. I had come quite a way from the hotel, so it was a long slog back.

I borrowed one of the Hotel facecloths and prepped Boris for his stickers. This led to me being summoned to reception and told I had to pay for a replacement cloth. I accepted my guilt and agreed to pay the nominal sum asked for.

Gregorio contacted me to say he was in town. The problem we have is Gregorio is a night owl and I am a morning man, so we struggle to connect. I was too tired for a late night, so I told him where I was going. He replied later saying he had done his own thing.

Another good rest and revival day concluded.

Monday 11/06/2018

Monday was a deliberate slow start for me. I had talked to the guy at reception yesterday and he told me he used to be a tour guide. I asked him what time would be best to leave from a traffic point of view and he said after 10am, maybe even 11am. I then told him I was thinking of going out to see the huge Genghis Khan statue. He strongly advised me against it, saying there is at least one road traffic death every week. As a man who skipped Machu Picchu, I had no issue taking his advice.

I set off after 11am with petrol anxiety as I had under 20 miles left in the tank and it was dropping like a stone based on the still quite heavy traffic. I finally spotted a petrol station but after crossing two busy lanes to get to the forecourt, I discovered it was closed. Still there was no need for my anxiety as within another mile I had multiple petrol stations to choose from.

A little further up the road the traffic was halted to allow a freight train to pass. I noticed some bikers ahead, so I weaved through the traffic to join them. They were ten Aussie bikers with a truck full of luggage and beer. I thought to myself "it will be good just to tag onto them for a while, who knows maybe even make camp." Two minutes later they turned south, and I turned north.

I had the coordinates for a wild camp site from the iOverlander app. This was the first time I had used it, so this would be interesting. This part of Mongolia was much greener and more populated. I preferred the rawness and wildness of the south. I was also surprised by the state of the road. This was the major route to Russia and it was pot-holed to a serious extent. Apparently, the roads that are being constructed are Chinese and low quality. Seems pointless to me.

It was a short ride today of under 200 miles so by around 5pm I was nearing my destination. The Sat Nav did its job and I was led onto a dirt/sand track that was pretty firm and after a mile or so I was at the spot. It seemed ideal with good flat ground amongst some trees and hidden from the highway. I enjoyed making camp and just as the tent was up the rain came on. Again, I was lucky with the timing of the rain. I sat it in the tent reading "Guy Martin," the only book I had carried and cooked my second and last camping food pack in the porch. I had visions of a cigar and a whisky to celebrate Mongolia, but I just didn't fancy it and I wasn't going to force it. As I drifted off, I thought I heard engine noise nearby but concluded it must have come from the highway.

Tuesday 12/06/2018

After a very restless early part of the night (anxiety attack.) I must have finally succumbed to fatigue as I awoke from a seriously deep sleep. It was bright outside and when I looked at my watch, I was surprised to discover it was 6am already. I was relived it was dry after last night's rain as there is nothing worse than packing up a tent in the wet. I unzipped the outer door and started my packing procedure. I pack all the inner contents first, away from any midges or mosquitos then quickly get the tent down and I'm away.

I started off down the track and just around the first bend I noticed two large over-lander trucks had also spent the night here. That engine noise I heard last night must have been them. I must admit I would have been quite alarmed if they had come around the corner last night with headlights blazing.

The track was damp but perfectly manageable, so I was soon back on the road. I was surprised that there was a town just a few miles on. I had imagined I was miles from anywhere last night. From there it was a decent drive to the next town which was on the border. To be honest the border crossing was great. Both the Mongolian and Russian sides seemed to prioritise and look after me. I had a little niggling worry if the codeine incident would flash up on a Russian border computer, but it was all good. Within a couple of hours, I was back in Russia.

As usual I was thinking in my helmet, this time about Mongolia. It was beautiful, ugly, raw, wild, scary and exciting. I had enjoyed the vast wilderness, I hated the food, I enjoyed most of the people but disliked the drunks. I would recommend you ride it with a lighter bike and a friend or two. I think more time to spend exploring the wild would be great, but I am so glad I came. My highlight had to be that day of hell followed by the desert camp. Didn't feel like it at the time.

The countryside on the road to Ulan-Ude was very pretty, reminding me of France. The roads were mainly good quality but even at their worst they were better than Mongolia. As I approached Ulan-Ude, I was surprised by how big it was. Thankfully the traffic was light as I rode into the city. After a bit of a detour due to closed streets, I finally arrived at the hotel. It was big, clean, very Soviet era but perfectly fine. I checked in then went straight out in search of food. I found a subway and had fun with the staff as they practiced their English on me. It was great to eat warm, tasty food.

I went back to the hotel for a sleep. When I woke, I felt really low. I know this sounds ridiculous but in town I noticed that there was a large number of western looking people and somehow, I translated this into they could speak English. Of course, I was wrong, they were Russian, just a different ethnicity. It just seemed like a long lonely haul on my own at that point.

I picked myself up and headed out for a light dinner which turned out to be good. While I was walking there, I noticed that there was a major event in the square. After dinner I was treated to a carnival atmosphere with quality live opera singers in the sunshine. It was made even more impressive with the huge stone carved Lenin head overlooking proceedings. It lifted my spirits no end. I found out later it was Russia day and a national holiday.

Wed 13/06/2018

Some of these older Russian hotels are vast and seem quite empty. Breakfast was served in a function hall with (bizarrely) two throne styled chairs perched at the end. The breakfast buffet qualifies as the worst hotel breakfast to date but better than yesterday's handful of nuts and raisins. After breakfast I took a leisurely stroll to Lenin Square where I was surprised to see the stage and barriers from last night had already been dismantled and shipped out. I stopped off for a coffee then wandered down the shopping area of Lenin street. My Russian phone sim was no longer working so I went into a Beeline shop where there was a girl who spoke a little English. My experience has been that it is mainly the girls who speak English. She told me I needed to top it up which I did with their help and I was on my way. I continued my search for the elusive Russian stickers for my bike but came up short.

On my way back to the hotel I noticed a guy wearing a tartan cap. As I walked past, I saw it said Scotland on the front. I smiled and said "I'm from Scotland." He spoke English and it turned out his daughter attended Glasgow University, so we had a good chat. I asked him if he was Russian and he responded that he was from the Republic of Buryatia. He said they had much in common with Scotland including sheep, meat as a main diet and while we had whisky, they had milk vodka. I guess you could add a sense of national identity to that.

My new friend – Ulan-Ude, Republic of Buryatia

The rest of the day was spent writing, relaxing, unsuccessful sticker hunting, finished off with a delicious Chicken Caesar Salad and a couple of beers in Churchill's pub in Lenin square.

Thursday 14/06/2018

Time to get moving.

I was up earlier than I needed to be, so it was a nice relaxed packing procedure. I had a little more leeway in my luggage space now which was good. Over the piece I had lost clothes, discarded clothes, dumped Tyre sealant and given a book to Alex. I hung around for the 7am breakfast then got on my way. The Sat Nav route out of town seemed strange as I ended up in small back streets. I stopped at a petrol station and while I was there did a quick check on my phone and I could see I was on the road to Chita. Quick is the key word here.

The road was reasonable for a while but then deteriorated. I remembered Alex had described the roads for a couple of days beyond Chita as being bumpy. "They must be really bad" I thought to myself. I rode for a few hours. I then hit a short gravel section which surprised me. It didn't last long and I was soon back on poor tarmac. Just outside of a town the road turned to gravel again but this time I probably rode for ten miles and there was no let up. I knew something was wrong, so I decided to backtrack to town where hopefully I had missed a turn.

I pulled into a petrol station on the edge of town. I had noticed all of the petrol stations were operated from behind a window box with no facilities or ability to go inside. It reminded me of off-licences in the rougher parts of Glasgow. There was a father and son just about to leave. I tried to ask him to wait until I got out my map, but they sped off. A few other people just shrugged their shoulders until finally a fully decked out Russian Orthodox Priest came to the rescue. We had no common language and the names on the map were in English, so it took quite a bit of pondering. Finally, he recognised and pointed to Sosnovo-

Ozerskoy my current location. He then pointed to the next town of Romanovka indicating that I needed to turn south there to Chita. I looked at the route I had travelled and in fact I had taken the B road. Unfortunately, there were no connecting roads so if I backtracked it would be all the way to the outskirts of Ulan-Ude. If I did that, I would lose a day but what lies ahead? I felt I had no choice but to move forward.

So off I went and for quite a while it was good gravel and I found myself operating mainly in fifth or six gear as compared to first and second in Mongolia. Half way to Romanovka the road deteriorated, so it was more third and fourth gear with occasional first and second. Even good gravel is a lot more tiring than tarmac. I kept praying for tarmac and about 15 miles out of town my prayers were answered. It was such a joy to relax again. "There is no way they would just pave this bit; it surely must stretch all 115 miles to Chita now," I thought to myself. I pulled into the petrol station and filled up. Once again, I was the star attraction in this very remote location.

As I pulled out of town, I saw the tarmac go into the horizon, I felt elated and relieved. Two miles later I felt completely dejected as the rough stuff returned with a vengeance. There were undulations and in the highs the mud was solid but, in the lows, it was wet and slippy. Sometimes I would get a break with longer higher stretches. There was no choice but keep moving forward. Thankfully I had no off's or even real near misses, I was getting better at this off-road riding.

I kept thinking "Ok this can't last for 99 miles, there has to be paved before then." Eventually with 25 miles to go the tarmac reappeared. Now I have had lots of false positives regarding tarmac in the trip. Sometimes they just tarmac the length of a village, however in this case it lasted all the way to Chita.

I was completely exhausted and hungry when I arrived at the hotel. I checked in as quick as you can in Russia then headed straight to the Irish Pub across the road for something to eat. I had hoped to watch the World Cup football that night, but I could not keep my eyes open.

Friday 15/06/2018

I woke up tired, but I knew I had another 500 miles ride today so needs must. I double checked the route and set off just after 7am. I stopped several times to make sure I was doing ok as I had my Garmin and Google maps going at the same time. Soon I was in the right road with no turns all the way to Erofey Pavlovich. I expected the scenery to be like what I had experienced in Finland or much of Sweden, road with trees up to the verges going on forever - it was not. Yes, there were many trees but also a lot of open space.

It was a trouble-free ride on great roads although it rained towards the end. The Erofey Pavlovich truckers stop was better than I had expected although bizarrely the lady would not give me a key so my door remained unlocked at all times. No worries though as I devised my own lock using straps from the bike. I unpacked Boris then went to a separate building for a shower. It took a bit of sign language and some smiles before the lady would let me in. I had not realised I had to pay separately for that. I then had a dinner of fish and rice in the trucker's café which was fine.

I was out doing a final check on Boris when three guys approached me. Two were Russian guides and the third an injured Korean biker. They explained he was with a group of 10 Korean riders, but he had fallen off. They had just organised the return of his badly damaged bike to Vladivostok. It must have been recent as his wrist was still weeping blood. He explained he had swapped lanes in roadworks failing to notice a change in level. I felt sorry for him as he explained that they were going all the way to Portugal, but he would now need to ride in the support car. Later that evening his friends all arrived just as I started to nod off in my room. All I can say is they were loud but regardless I was fast asleep by 8pm.

Saturday 16/06/2018

Oh, how good it was to feel fresh that morning. I had bought a couple of mini muffins in the shop the previous evening so after devouring one of them I was good to go. It was just after 6am and dry but cloudy. I felt a huge positive difference in energy from yesterday, I was up for this 495-mile ride to Khabarovsk. I did my usual countdown. Get to 400, then 299, then 200, then 156, then 100, then 50 then 21 and arrive. 200 is a Xmas day double return run to my parents' home in New Cumnock, 100 is a single return run and 50 is one way. 156 is the distance from New Cumnock to Blackpool where my parents took us on holiday each year. I always sing "we're all going on our summer holidays" at that point. 21 is New Cumnock to Ayr which was my motorcycle commute as a boy.

I stopped a few times, refuelled Boris and had some food on the go for myself. The rain started with about 300 miles to go and never really let up after that. It became very heavy in the final 100 miles as I rode through what looked like paddy fields to me. The countryside was really adopting this Chinese border theme.

When I arrived in Khabarovsk it was monsoon style rain and the streets were like rivers in some places. I was seriously concerned Boris' engine would get flooded. We made it to the hotel, but I got further soaked in the unpacking process.

A surly security guard asked me to move my bike. He walked me into what looked like disused underground parking but it was dry, so I was grateful in the end. I had noticed on the road that my rear tyre was a little soft, so I set about blowing it up and drying out the inside of the panniers. I felt good that was done. This trip was a real test of physical and mental endurance.

I discovered my iPhone had gotten very wet. The screen was all distorted and it was boiling hot. I left it to dry hoping it would be ok in the morning. I looked for dinner options and found there was only one in the hotel but with this rain it would have to do. It was Chinese which was appropriate as the Chinese city of Heihe is on the other side of the river. It was actually quite tasty although asking for the beer options brought an interesting response. "We have green, yellow or black was the reply."

Sunday 17/06/2018

I had a decent sleep despite being disturbed by a presumably drunken husband trying to get Stella to open the room door. Stella was the only word I understood but I think I got it right.

He would be in bother in the morning I would imagine. I checked my iPhone and it was dead. Based on what I read a replacement battery might work. I would try and check that out in Vladivostok. I moved the bike outside the hotel and packed up. I had another bad breakfast but I did get a great view of the river with the Chinese town of Heihe on the other side. I could not resist saying "hello old China" which was an old Glasgow way of greeting a friend.

I checked out as they were holding a 2,000 roubles deposit. "We need to charge you for the condoms" said the young receptionist. "I only opened the box because I thought they were sweets or playing cards. I didn't use them," I replied a tad embarrassed. "You opened them, so you must pay 100 roubles" she replied.

After picking up my 1900 roubles I was on my way. Thankfully it was a sunny morning and the streets were mainly dry. I stopped off for petrol before heading out of town. This time I had no choice but trust the Sat Nav as I had no phone as an alternative. The other major issue was the map, I had listed place names in English only while the road signs were in Cyrillic. Always buy a map with both would be my advice.

The Sat Nav did me proud although it was a convoluted route along scary industrialised back roads, before I finally reached the highway. By that time, I had covered over 130 miles with around 300 to go. The highway was great, snaking through some more undulating hills with lots of trees but also lots of green space. For the first time in the trip I could see the Trans-Siberian railway was running parallel to my right.

The ride to Khabarovsk was stress free and after three fuel and rest stops, I was soon crossing the Amur river and heading into town. I found the hotel with ease and was checked in before 5pm. I noted that I had crossed my final time zone – 9 hours ahead of the UK. I was now n the same time-zone as Sydney, Australia.

Khabarovsk had a nice centre with an impressive Church. The hotel was very plush and close to the main street filled with modern stores. I looked around and was excited to discover an iPhone repair shop. The guy confirmed it had water damage (I knew that) but said it would take 2 days to look at it.

That evening I visited the Harley Davidson bar which was good, but I didn't see any reference to Harley Davison on the inside. After that I had a FaceTime call with my parents to wish my dad happy Father's Day. The connection was lost before I was able to say the words. I ended the evening with another tyre top-up session. Thank goodness for my little battery driven pump. It worked a treat!

Monday 18/06/2018

Vladivostok Awaits!

I decided not to hang about for breakfast at 7am that morning, I was too eager to get going. The road out of town was trouble free and I soon found myself on the main route again. The countryside was green with some rolling hills and trees. It could have been Germany or even England. It seemed much more fertile here and I guess that's why there was a lot more habitation. During the journey I was never that far from the next settlement and petrol stations were plentiful. It was at one of those petrol stations I decided to top up my rear tyre pressure again. During this process I noticed the root cause of the issue. There was a nail embedded deep in my tyre. I had a slight panic to start with but then remembered I had already ridden about 1500 miles on it so there should be no reason I cannot do another 300. I put the pressure to 3.0 bar and monitored my tyre pressure sensor in the dashboard. It ran for 100 miles before dropping 0.2 bar, so it was good.

The ride seemed long today, well actually it was long at 475 miles, but still I had done that in previous days. It was now all about arriving safely at my final target. I stopped about 50 miles or so outside Vladivostok and emptied my petrol cans into the tank. I should not be needing them now. Just after that the rain came on, not torrential like the other day but constant. I pulled over again to zip up my air vents then continued into the city.

It was very busy, so it was a slow final 6 miles before I eventually arrived at my targeted destination. Tokarev Lighthouse which was very unimpressive as a lighthouse but that didn't matter. Boris and I were at trails end East on the edge of the Pacific Ocean (the Sea of Japan). I got some random guy to take some photos and chatted to a couple of Australian blokes. It was great to have someone to share my enthusiasm with. "We did it Boris!" I said patting the petrol tank.

Trails End – The Sea of Japan (Pacific Ocean) – Vladivostok - Russia

It was a 4-mile ride to the hotel and on arrival I parked up beside the Rusmototravel bikes in the car park. The return tour was due to go the following morning or so I thought. There were no sign of participants or guides at all that evening. I located the BMW dealer on the iPad, so I could go get my tyre looked at the following day. I decided that was a better option than trying to plug it myself as the nail head was below the surface and would need digging out.

I also rechecked the shipping company instructions to put the coordinates into the GPS. I noticed Alex had listed two sets of coordinates. One was for the shipping company the other said for signing papers. This really worried me. What did he mean, was it a government office? If yes, I was sure there could be many offices around that location and how would I communicate. I sent him a mail asking for clarity but with the time difference it could be a while before I get a response.

I walked into the city centre and had some food then had an early night, but I must admit I felt frustrated I was still in a world of worry rather than a world of relaxation.

Tuesday 19/06/2018

I was in the host country of World Cup 2018 and I had not watched a match. Easier said than done though as due to the time difference games were mainly played in the early hours of the morning. That morning I caught the second half of Brazil versus Switzerland which ended in a 1-1 draw.

I went down to reception and asked them if they could type the address for the BMW dealer into my Garmin which they did. It didn't look right as it was only showing as 7 miles away. I was convinced it was further than that. I got them to enter another couple of other bike repair places as a backup. I had a look at the map on my iPad and noticed the Botanical Gardens were showing as being across the road from the BMW place. I managed to find that in the Garmin local attractions. I also entered the coordinates Alex had provided for Trans Trek the freight company.

I went outside and inflated the rear tyre once more. Still no sign of any Rusmototravel guys. Just after 9am I got ready to go with a positive mindset. I assumed I could get the tyre fixed, then I would go straight to the freight company and leave Boris. As I followed the directions for the BMW place I started pondering if

I should forget it and go to the freight place and ride home with Norman the nail. Thankfully I decided that was a stupid idea. I got to where the BMW place should be and as expected it wasn't, so I did a U-turn and landed in city commuter traffic. I selected the Botanical gardens and noticed it was on the same road I had been on only further out. That made sense, maybe the street number is wrong on the BMW website. I did another U-turn and 5 miles or so up the road the dealership emerged from the mist on my left.

Another U-turn later and I was riding into the dealer and parked up. I entered the bike section and saw a guy at a desk. "Do you speak English? I need your help," I said with a smile. "Yes," he replied and shook my hand then said, "We met in Mongolia right?" I could not believe it; he was one of the three Russians who had reassured me I was on the right road and whom I rode with for a short while. His name was Grigory and he was brilliant. He told me he would get the tyres swapped right away and took me for a coffee. I was so relieved and so grateful I had persevered. Boris came back shining like a new pin with the Tourance tyres refitted. I gave Grigory the Anekee Wild tyres as there was still life in them, and I had no need for them. He applied a couple of great stickers to Boris and I was on my way.

I had managed to check my mail in the BMW shop and I had a response from Alex regarding the two sets of coordinates for shipping the bike which clarified nothing. He was more or less saying "I don't know why you are worried." Clearly, we were having a lost in translation moment. Regardless I headed back into the city feeling great and made straight for the first coordinates for Trans Trek. It was a strange looking place and there was no sign of a freight company. I walked around and asked a few people, but I was stumped. I typed the second set in and it showed 500 metres away but still nothing. That's when it twigged that the two sets of coordinates might both be Trans Trek. I decided to go back to the hotel and get an address from the internet and get reception to type it in.

I left the hotel hoping the Garmin would not lead me to the same place. I was thinking contingency if it did. I could get reception to call them and send a taxi for me to follow. Anyway, the Garmin led me to the right place and with no common language but lots of smiles we got the job done. It involved a guy leading me from an office a few hundred metres to the rail depot (not a station). I had to take the panniers, top box and windscreen off then disconnect the battery. This was all done with about 6 guys laughing and joking about whisky and William Wallace. I then went into the office where a bunch of friendly ladies completed paperwork for me to sign, made me a coffee and ordered a taxi. It was a proper old-style office with a good atmosphere. The taxi came, and I was on my way.

I felt I could finally relax at last. When I arrived at the hotel there was a couple of guys at the Rusmototravel bikes. I could not believe it; it was the two Australians I had met at the Lighthouse. They confirmed they were doing the ride to Moscow and they told me that they had not mentioned it as it was my moment. Another amazing coincidence and two very thoughtful guys.

I sorted out my stuff for packing then walked around town. I had another go at getting my iPhone fixed. The guys in this little shop tried really hard but, in the end, they couldn't fix it. I also did some scouting for a suitcase or bag for the flight. I located some expensive options then decided to look again the next day. After that it was dinner and another early night. During my walk I absolutely concurred with the description of Vladivostok being the San Francisco of the East. Fog, steep hills, bridges and multicultural people.

Wednesday 20/06/2018

My last day in the Far East.

The morning started with me seeing off the Rusmototravel guys on their trip. They were all geared up and ready to go, awaiting the late arrival of an Austrian guy. I felt their frustration although no-one said anything. The Austrian guy turned up and I took a group photo of them and they were on their way. I did not envy them in the least.

I had mapped out a walking route around town to catch the sites such as the Railway Station which had been recommended and a Submarine. I enjoyed strolling at my leisure picking up a good coffee at a kiosk on the way. Not sure if I was in the right part of the railway station but it did not seem too special to me. The U boat on the other hand was special as it had been literally placed on the pavement on a main thoroughfare. It dated from the Second World War and was a big sucker.

The sun had finally come out in Vladivostok so that made the wandering all the more pleasurable. I finally bit the bullet on an overpriced suitcase as I had no other choice really. I was thinking that I wished I was flying that day but in reality, if that had been the case, I would have been in panic mode yesterday.

I had an early dinner that night and finished off the Vlad experience with a couple of Russian cocktails made up by the friendly bar owner.

Thursday 21/06/2018

The taxi was on time at 5am and for a mere £18, I was whisked what seemed like a long way to the airport. The rain had come back with a vengeance and there was some flooding on the highway. I was glad I was not on the bike.

When I had checked in yesterday, I was delighted to see Aeroflot had a relationship with KLM, so based on my membership level earned in pervious employment I was given priority check-in and lounge access. The airport was very bright and modern, and the signs were in Russian and English. The check-in desks were not open initially but when they did, I whizzed through the priority lane. Security went smoothly and soon I was in the lounge relaxing before being called for the flight.

I had a window seat with a similar aged couple occupying the middle and the aisle. Unfortunately, the wife liked sitting at an angle which encroached on my space. Even worse she took off her shoes and propped up her bare feet. That combined with heavy motorcycle trousers would make for a long 8-hour flight. There's a thought. I had ridden my bike such a distance from a Moscow that it was taking 8 hours on a 777 to get back, wow.

A few sleeps and movies later we finally landed at Moscow's SVO airport which unfortunately was on the opposite side of the city from my hotel near DME, my departure airport. I had researched trains etc but during the flight had decided I would pay up to £50 for a taxi just to make life easier with all the bike gear etc. On exit I looked for an official taxi desk to get a price. There was a Yandex desk which is the Russian equivalent of Uber. The guy spoke English and very efficiently came up with a fixed price of 2200 roubles which is around £25 for a two-hour journey. I was delighted and was soon on my way. Two hours later I was at my Airport hotel and spent the afternoon watching Denmark versus Australia play in the World Cup, trying to stay awake which I did until 6pm.

Friday 22/06/2018

I had arranged for the shuttle to leave at 03:30am but since I was up, I left at 03:00am. I located the BA desk and was checked in and through security quite quickly. I had a that niggling worry that there may be an issue with either leaving the bike or my drugs incident. Having passed two passport check points and security before reaching the gates I heaved a sigh of relief. Unfortunately, they had another full passport check beyond all that. The young lady took ages which made me twitch but finally I was waved through.

I had stripped the armour out of my bike trousers which made quite a difference in weight and comfort. This combined with a short three-and-a-half-hour flight made for a far more comfortable experience. I spent nearly £14 on a full breakfast and Americano at Heathrow and did not grudge a penny. The Glasgow flight was slightly delayed but soon I was on my way. Amber was waiting to whisk me home and thus end the trip. I still needed to repatriate Boris though.

Repatriation of Boris

After a whirlwind weekend I found myself back at work. It was hard but manageable. The real difference between this trip and the last big one was that this time I felt both physically and mentally exhausted. The Mongolian desert and those last series of long rides had taken it out of me. At that point the thought of returning and riding Boris back from Moscow was very unappealing. Slowly but surely both my mental and physical strength improved.

A week before I was due to return, Alex confirmed Boris was back with him in Moscow and in good shape. I reconfirmed the arrangements; he would park him in the Bagration Hotel ready for a fast exit. A couple of days before I set off, Dirk the Dutchman contacted me to say he was flying in early on the Friday and planning to leave at 6am. This trip was full of meet-up coincidences as that was exactly when I was planning to leave. I called him and offered to ride together which he seemed keen on. We agreed to keep in touch over the next couple of days.

Thursday 12/07/2018

From misery to happiness as the Proclaimers song goes. I woke up looking forward to collecting Boris. The flights via Heathrow were on time and before I knew it, I was landing in Moscow on a gloriously sunny evening. I took a cab to avoid sweating in my bike suit on a train and arrived back at the familiar Bagration Hotel. I scanned the car park for Boris and eventually spied him hidden under a black bike cover. It was so good to see him in one piece. Actually, he was in several pieces with the battery, mirrors, windscreen and luggage detached.

I quickly checked in, changed my trousers, grabbed my keys and got straight into re-assembly. First of all, I connected the battery and fired him up. It was a joy to hear him roar into life. Then it was time to fit the screen, mirrors and luggage.

As I was finishing off, I noticed a bunch of bikes arrive. "Surely not," I thought to myself, but it was. The guys I had waved off in Vladivostok were riding in to end their trip. Alex II smiled at me and shook his head. "Hey you are everywhere," he said. I congratulated them and took their group photo just as I had in Vladivostok. They had made it safely but sadly the Austrian guy who had been late that first morning had a bad crash and was hospitalised before returning home part way into the trip.

I was determined to get an early sleep as I we had an early departure, so I declined a late dinner invite from the guys and headed out to a place we had visited last time. I had a delicious burger and chips and enjoyed some chat with French football fans excited about Sunday's final. That night Dirk messaged me confirming he was on his way and we would meet at 6am.

Friday 13/07/2018

Bye bye Russia.

I was up by 4am, so took the time to get organised for the off. I assumed Dirk may be a little late as you never know with airports etc. I plugged in the directions in my Sat Nav and discovered I did not have my Russian maps loaded. This may get interesting if Dirk does not show up. I downloaded Moscow google maps on my (new) phone as a contingency.

I wandered down at our 6am agreed rendezvous time and was delighted to see Dirk rolling in. I told him to take his time as we were not in a rush. He had little to do other than change his trousers and throw a bag on the bike. We set off not long after 6am with the first priority being a fuel stop as our bikes had to have minimal fuel for rail transportation. Moscow was nice and quiet, and the petrol station was located just by the ramp to our exit highway.

I was a bit worried about my comfort levels for these long rides. I had woken up with a sore tail bone the week previous which made for uncomfortable sitting. The prospect of several 490 mile plus days was interesting. The journey to the border was trouble free as it's basically a straight road. Dirk led the way and was only stopping when we needed fuel - after around 180 miles or so. My bum was on fire for most of the journey but at a manageable and constant pain level. I stood up regularly to ease things off.

We arrived at the border at 1:30pm which was great timing. The Russian side went fairly smoothly and efficiently but the Latvian side was slow and painful. In the end we were there for over three hours. I have two observations:

1. It doesn't have to be like that in today's high-tech world.
2. Border staff give you the first impression of a country. I rode into Latvia feeling very negative based on the attitude of some of the staff.

Thankfully that evening we were treated well by the hotel and restaurant staff which helped cure my negative impression. Still Latvia, take a look at your border set-up.

Saturday 14/07/2018

We skipped breakfast and were on the road just after 6am. It was rainy and miserable, but the roads were good. I grabbed a snickers bar at our first fuel stop which served as breakfast - Dirk seemed to survive without food. We continued through Latvia and into Lithuania where we had another fuel stop. I screwed up on translation and instead of a black coffee I ordered a sweet hot chocolate which I grudgingly drank. We had a late lunch stop just before the Polish border where we were served by a very angry young Lithuanian lady.

We entered Poland and rode on to our final destination of Lomza. The rain came back again as we entered the town and before too long, we found the Amadeus Hotel. I sensed Dirk was feeling it was too early to stop. I guess I could have done some more but as my hotel was booked and paid for; I was sticking to plan.

We parked up and entered the hotel just behind a young couple with a kid checking in for the evening. The young male receptionist dealt with them then turned unenthusiastically to us. We explained I had a reservation, but Dirk needed a room. "There are no spare rooms as we have a wedding party tonight," he said almost gleefully. Dirk turned to me, shook my hand and said he was moving on. It was all very sudden, but I think that suited him and I was ok with it as well. He had been great company and I wished him a safe journey.

The hotel room was compact but fine and I found myself a good little pizza place to chill for dinner. I had to sleep with earplugs in that night to dampen the music from the wedding reception.

Sunday 17/07/2018

The longest ride.

The morning started badly as I dropped Boris in the car park after losing balance as I pushed him off his centre stand. I was angry with myself as I picked him up.

I hate when I could have prepared better. I had a 537 miles ride in front of me and here I was faffing about a rainy town in Poland not trusting the Sat Nav for no real reason. My assumption was I would hit highway straight away, but I was mistaken. By the time I had followed signs and taken diversions, I had turned a 537 miles ride into 550. Eventually I decided to trust the device and go with the flow, enjoying the rural countryside to the best of my ability in the pouring rain. At least it was tarmac and good tarmac at that.

I eventually popped out into the highway and with a yell of delight I was haring towards Warsaw. I made my way through the city and was heading east before I reached the magical "400 miles to go" mark. The clouds had cleared and the sun was drying me off. Time to celebrate with a breakfast McMuffin and a black coffee. I then persevered on with the constant throb of a sore bum. I was worried about roadworks on the Berlin ring road, but the traffic kept on flowing. It did come to a halt later due to an accident but as I was hot, tired and sore I boldly filtered my way past tooting my horn and revving my engine to create room.

I was a very happy man to see the Helmstedt exit and even happier to see such a nice comfortable Best Western hotel. It was around 4pm and I rushed into the room to get cleaned up and watch the World Cup final. I was rooting for Croatia as they were the underdogs. I asked the receptionist if there was somewhere, I could watch it and she pointed to a little gathering of empty chairs by a TV. I had envisioned watching it with a bunch of enthusiastic Germans, but I guess they weren't interested. Still I enjoyed the match, if not the result and chilled that evening.

Monday 16/07/2018

I awoke just before 6am with a debate in my head. Do I leave now and get through Hannover early or do I wait till 8:30am and leave later? I had a room, Wi-Fi and breakfast being served downstairs. Both would get me to the ferry on plenty of time, what was there to debate? Well you see it's me and movement; I really struggle to sit still when I could be moving but thankfully common sense kicked in. In saying that, I still went to the stage of getting geared up and opening my room door before concluding "this is crazy."

I set off just after 8:30am and had a fairly clear run on a warm sunny morning. There was a hold up at one point due to a truck crash, but I filtered through it all. I could not believe how good the German drivers were for making space. I enjoy Germany and, in most cases, enjoy German people even although they always queue jump at borders. I was happy in myself that morning. I stopped for a coffee and an Ice Cream after entering the Netherlands by way of celebration, I was nearly there, sore bum and all. A few hours later I had negotiated the Amsterdam ring road and I was in Ijemum, the ferry port town. First things first, a detour to Albert Hiejn (Dutch Supermarket) to buy some soft and salty liquorice for Amber then a stop at a fresh fish shop for a roll with salad and fresh herring - sounds bad but it was delicious. I then rode down to the ship and after passing security was waved straight on. As I had learned from the last time, I was waiting for the doors to open in the buffet restaurant getting ahead of the masses. Great food and a relaxing time was had.

Tuesday 17/07/2018

I woke up after a really good sleep aided by the gentle rocking of the ship. I was down just before the 7am opening time for the breakfast buffet, it was mobbed. I knew I had blown it. This is why I had stopped ordering breakfast buffets. I had managed to get around the evening chaos by being insanely early but that was not possible with breakfast. It's not the quality of the food, it's the swarms of pushy humans that makes it a grind for me. I ate up as soon as I could and headed out. On the way to the cabin I decided to take a look at the coffee bar. Quiet, comfy chairs and just what the doctor ordered. I grabbed a proper coffee and relaxed, enjoying the peace and quiet.

The ferry docked on time, but it took a while before they opened the doors. It was a dry day as I rolled off the ferry, which was fortunate because we were made to queue for over half an hour at passport control.

I rode out of the port and straight into roadworks which was annoying. After clearing the roadworks, I was finally in the Northumbrian countryside heading north. The rain came on intermittently as I snaked through the gentle rolling hills and before long I was cheering as I crossed the border into Scotland at Coldstream. From there it was a bum aching ride back home.

Since leaving the house back in May, Boris had clocked up another 10,800 miles. What a bike!

Interim Report

I was asked in a regular basis "how was it?" My answer is always "hard" followed by "it was definitely an adventure, not a holiday." I feel the same thing as I am writing this now. I have clearer memories of hard times than good times. When I say hard times, I mean not only the really hard times like the Gobi Desert but the sheer distances that needed to be covered. I am glad I did it, but I have no desire to do it again. There were brilliant highlights such as Moscow, the Russian Altai and Mongolia which all surpassed expectations. I can also now look back and say the Gobi Desert was the most memorable experience with the highlight being the forced camp.

I appreciate everyone does things their own way, but I would recommend you have at least one riding mate in Mongolia. Not only would have been great for picking up the bikes but it would have given me more confidence to ride faster in the sand and to explore more. In saying that I would not advocate you need a riding partner everywhere. I enjoyed the freedom on many parts of the trip.

Successful learnings from the last trip were:

- Light packing with no bag strapped to my seat.
- My laminated suit negating the need to carry waterproofs saved space and hassle.
- My free-standing tent was a must for the rocky Gobi Desert.
- Carrying tyres (this time well secured with Roc Straps) gave me comfort and security and ultimately, they were used.
- Carry a couple of emergency camping meals
- Always have a fruit/nut mix and water in your top box.

Boris was serviced and MOT'd by Craig at Racin n Cruisin and all was well other than the Centre Stand was hanging off. That could have been interesting. What a bike!

I glance up at the map with a black line plotting my route and feel a sense of achievement. I look at the gap "West to East" across the America's. I smile at the prospect of closing the gap.

Preparation Part 2

September brought me my first grandchild. Corey Brown Wilson, a beautiful little boy to my daughter Stephanie and her husband Scott. It is a wonderful feeling to be a grandfather. I brought him a little bib with Born to be Wild from the Thunder in the Glens rally in Aviemore. I certainly won't be pushing him towards motorbikes but would not try to (couldn't) stop him if he goes in that direction. Same with my children. Riding bikes brings danger and to be honest I would worry about the influence I had created. A bit two faced from such a passionate biker I know. September also brought the engagement of my youngest son Liam to his girlfriend Gilzian. It looked like there may be two weddings in 2019 as my eldest son Justin and his partner Hazel were already getting married in July that year.

Ok onto preparation. I would need freight, flights, travel and bike insurance. Thankfully no Visa's just an ESTA. Boris shouldn't need much more than a service and a fresh set of tyres. I have no gear to buy. Sounded scarily straightforward.

I called Moto Freight to check on costs and options. Once again, I received great service. Kathy from Moto Freight provided me with air freight quotes into Seattle and Vancouver and sea freight from New York. They were in line with my expectations. The sea freight was Kathy's suggestion and at around 2/3 of the cost of air freight, it made sense. I was moving towards picking Seattle as my departure point to avoid any potential cross border insurance issues. The sea freight solution now pointed towards me finishing in New York.

I had been hoping to have Amber either travel with me for the last few miles of the trip or be there at my destination. Based on this I started looking at options in or around NYC. Montauk lighthouse at the end of Long Island quickly became the favourite. The problem would be getting Amber there. I identified a hotel some 50 miles or so from NYC and 45 miles from the lighthouse. I could ride to the hotel, get a bus to JFK, hire a car, bring Amber to the hotel, then ride together to the lighthouse. I would then need to drive her back to NYC, drop off the car, get a bus back, drop my bike at the sea freight terminal then get into NYC. Amber would also have to bring bike gear. It was all sounding complicated.

I then looked at just getting her to get into the city alone and meet her at a point. Ewan and Charlie had finished at Battery Park, maybe that could work. On further investigation I found I could not stop there on the bike. 9/11 had changed things. I asked her if she was ok if I finished my trip alone, dropped off the bike and picked her up at JFK. She said she was happy with that if I was. It sounded like the best plan.

Around the same time, I had been in touch with Mark, the American on the Rusmototravel trip. He had misunderstood my update on the trip and assumed I was starting from San Francisco. He said they would make sure I had a bed available. That got me thinking so I contacted Moto Freight and found that freight costs were £100 cheaper too. I had a new departure point.

I was also reconsidering my end-point. Maybe I should end the trip in Boston and leave the bike there for the winter, then take another ride the following year to get best buy for my freight and insurance costs. You might be thinking I keep changing my plans, but this is how it works for me, a trip evolves.

My last planned overnight ride of 2018 was an October trip to the Red Squirrel in Glencoe. I love Glencoe, with its foreboding mountains and dark history. I love the Red Squirrel campsite but only on off season when the tourists and midges have left. It is in a spectacular setting and with a short walk to the Clahaig Inn and its excellent selection of real ales.

I had been in semi-regular contact with Graham, the Englishman living in Aberdeen who was on the Rusmototravel trip. We had made a couple of failed attempts to meet up due to my work commitments but this time we could both make it. Hutch also decided to take this late season overnighter opportunity.

I started work early that Friday and by 3pm I was on the road. We had stumbled into a short relatively good weather window in what had been a very rainy period. The ride up was enjoyable but only after clearing what I considered was a very busy Glasgow for that time of day. I did not make any stops so within a couple of hours I was pulling up in the campsite. I spotted Hutch and

Graham's bikes parked next to their tents in a prime spot near the river with a glorious view. Hutch was finishing off his unpacking process while Graham had headed off for a shower. They had introduced themselves and before long Graham came back with a smile and a warm greeting. It was a strange feeling to think the last time I had seen him was waving him and his bike off in Novosibirsk.

Hutch handed us a beer just as the rain came on, so we all retired to our tents to let the shower pass. After 15 minutes or so it stopped so we agreed to make our way to the Clahaig. We had a great night in the pub reminiscing about Russia and filling in the gaps when we were apart. I was keen to move the subject along to avoid Hutch feeling left out and bored. Graham would be 70 next year and was clearly determined to make the most of his good health. I could almost sense a little fear and desperation to get things done with old age looming. He was trying to convince us to take a Road of Bones trip with Rusmototravel next year, but I had my plans and Hutch did not fancy it. He was also trying to tempt me into a ride through Africa. I had said it was a step too far but underneath it all I was thinking "maybe."

We took the opportunity to toast the birth of wee Corey.

After a few rounds we called it a night and headed back to the campsite to have a whisky and in my case a cigar by the campfire. A great night was had.

After a good sleep we took a slow start on a cold morning then made our way towards Oban stopping off at the Castle Stalker Café for a delicious breakfast. Graham gave us a hug and headed north while Hutch and I headed south taking the great bikers road through Oban, Lochgilphead, Inveraray towards Loch Lomond. We split up by Balloch and I headed home after a very enjoyable trip.

In November I bit the bullet and booked our flights and a Boston hotel. My son Liam had confirmed his wedding would take place on 24th of August so I would leave for San Francisco on the 26th. Both Amber and I would return from Boston on the 22nd of September in time for Corey's first birthday. My planned finish date was on Sunday the 15th of September at the Aquarium in Boston. Amber would fly out a few days before to acclimatise.

Boston holds a dear place in my heart as I visited many times while I worked for Digital Equipment Corporation over a 23-year period. It was a fantastic company to work for and it had a major positive influence in my life, both financially and socially. Raymond, Hutch and Moose also worked there.

I wrote to Tracy, an ex Digital colleague who lives close to Boston and he kindly said he would find a place to store my bike and big Mark confirmed he would host me in San Francisco. I also let Moto Freight know the dates. The flights were with KLM and came in at just under £1000 for both which was well within my budget estimate. Boston hotels were very pricy but after much searching, I found a Doubletree Hilton a little out of the centre but close to the T (Subway).

On November 28th I called my mother to confirm an online grocery order I was placing for her. The call was answered by a paramedic, my 87-year-old dad had collapsed, and it was serious. I called my brother who was local, and he rushed to their side. I left work in Edinburgh and made my way to pick up Amber in Glasgow then onwards towards New Cumnock. On route my brother Ian informed me they had him breathing again and he was going to Ayr hospital and we should meet him there. He said it was bad. I go into what I call an operational mode when under stress, where I just keep going. Soon after arriving at the hospital a doctor informed us that he had a heart attack and had stopped breathing for 15 minutes. Somehow his heart and breathing had restarted but he was very weak and most certainly brain damaged. It was only a matter of time. We were allowed to go to his side where we spent a distressing six hours seeing his body struggling away until he finally was at peace. He was a good man who lead a good life and we will all miss him dearly.

In the early days my mother and father had resisted my desire to get a bike despite having owned a Frances Barnett himself. They finally gave in and he helped me collect and maintain my BSA Bantam. He took me a memorable ride on it down to Galloway before I turned 17, stopping off at a café in Newton Stewart. I put my parents through hell by my reckless riding over the next few years before maturing into family life. His mind faded over the last few years, so he was never really connected to what I was doing on my trips. I am sure as a younger man he would have been fascinated and proud of me. That's the thought I will carry forward.

During December I turned my thoughts to my route planning. I like to have at least an outline plan, but it would be open to change based on weather condition or advice given on the road. My most likely route would be to head out to Reno Nevada where I would join route 50 "America's loneliest road." I had thought about a route via Pikes Peak in Colorado as suggested by Hutch. This is where they have an annual race up the mountain. It appealed to me but with the death of my father I was now drawn further north to Lakota territory. He had a lifelong interest in the history and culture of Native Americans and in particular, the plains tribes. We had toured some of that area by car but there was still plenty unseen. I fancied passing through Sturgis, South Dakota, home of the famous annual motorcycle rally - although I would miss that by a few weeks. Another potential target would be the Indian Motorcycle factory in Spirit Lake in Iowa. Why there you may ask? I loved the Indian brand for many years but the bikes were always way out of reach financially. Then came Polaris who, in my opinion have done a brilliant job of resurrecting the brand with some stunning bikes. When they reintroduced the Scout, it was too hard to resist.

I requested to go from full time employment at my work down to 4 days a week and it was accepted. With that, January started off with a series of Monday Munro outings with Hutch. A Munro is a Scottish mountain with a height of 3,000 feet or more. There are 282 in total and those who climb them are known as Munro baggers. I must admit I love doing them. You get to places you would never go, take in spectacular views and its great exercise. At the time of writing this I had completed 41 so still a way to go.

There was talk of a Croatia bike trip in 2020. Hutch was the driver with Tree and Kenny very keen. I liked the idea but wondered how it might affect my plans of leaving Boris out in the USA. I could make that final decision i.e. leave him or bring him home straightaway nearer the time. It would involve an away day at the end to drop him in New York, but Amber was cool with that.

The other interesting find in January was my discovery that people had been finding it impossible to insure foreign bikes in the USA. Now that could be a trip killer but it seems as if it is resolved for now with a company named Progressive Insurance providing policies. I would certainly arrange insurance before committing to shipping the bike.

In February I sent a four-week holiday proposal to my boss. I would carry over one week, buy one week and take two weeks of this year's holiday allocation. My workmate John had agreed to cover for me. Thankfully, as I had booked the flights, it was approved. I could now announce it on my Facebook book group (Once around the Block – by Motorcycle), it was official!

March saw me do further insurance checks. My normal holiday travel insurance looked as if it may cover me with the exception of personal liability. I mulled over this then decided to take no risks, so I opted for Navigator Motorcycle Gold cover. That would cover me but not the bike. For bike insurance I did an online quote using my friends US address with Progressive Insurance. Third party only cover came in at an impressive $80 for a year. I decided to wait until May before kicking it off as you can only start it 60 days in advance and I may need it next year. I had started the thought process around where I might go next year if I did leave the bike to get more value out of the freight. I got very excited for a while about the Trans-Labrador Highway in eastern Canada. Another adventurous trip on gravel roads through wilderness, routing back south using ferries. I threw a teaser out to Graham to see if he would be interested in joining me. He didn't bite. Maybe a more relaxed ride down the spine of the Appalachian Mountains would be a better bet on my own.

May brought my 60th birthday and some nice family celebrations around it. I had two bike camping trips planned in May; the first was an island hopper trip taking in North and South Uist and Barra. Callum at Saltire Motorcycles in Edinburgh had offered me the opportunity to take one of his bikes for an extended test ride. Initially he was thinking of one of the big Indians such as the Chieftain but the demo bikes were late in arriving. I had mentioned I would love to try the new KTM 790 Adventure, so we settled on that. I must admit I felt a little strange even unfaithful not taking my own bike but I was looking forward to it. The island hopper trip was brilliant and I must admit so was the bike. Light, powerful and handled like a dream. Scotland once again delivered a brilliant bike camping experience. The islands were as varied as the weather with rugged hills, flat peat bogs and white sandy beaches.

The second trip annual trip was traditionally taken by myself and my good friend Moose Kerr (another ex-Digital colleague). Over the year's participation has ebbed and flowed but this year was well attended. Participants were Moose, Tree, Hutch, wee Martin, Kenny and myself. As usual I took Moose on Boris and we all rendezvoused at the Green Welly in Tyndrum for breakfast. Friday was very rainy so the pub was location of choice from mid-afternoon onwards. Saturday was a better weather day allowing Hutch and I to do our first Munro (Ben More) using a motorcycle to get to the starting point and back. Sunday was very wet on the island but dried off to make it a pleasant ride home.

May also brought the news that I would be made redundant on July 4th. This came as a bit of a surprise but in the end, it was the impetus I needed to get on with retirement. My trip was budgeted and there would be no impact other than more leisure time at either end.

I had a couple of issues develop with Boris during this time period. Firstly, my fuel gauge failed. I was aware of the poorly designed fuel strip in this model but it had lasted me ten years so no complaints. The second issue was my tyre pressure sensors started to fail.

After some research I discovered the batteries in the sensors usually expire after five or six years so again no complaints. As usual, fixing BMW'S can be expensive so I checked google for options. I discovered a potential fix for the fuel strip which involved sending an electrical charge using an adapted lighter to weld the fault. I talked to Craig at Racin n Cruisin and he knew exactly what I was describing and had the tool to try it. I was amazed to discover that it worked, although it only lasted for a month so I bit the bullet and had BMW fit a new strip with a 2-year warranty.

I did the same research on the tyre sensors and discovered that a guy successfully dug out the irreplaceable batteries and replaced and resealed them. I gave it a go with some help from Craig but again it failed after a short while. Another BMW fix with a 2-year warranty was the answer.

In early July I left the bike with Craig and a "Craig List." This was far shorter than previous lists:

Oil and Filter Change
Alternator belt change {Craig's suggestion)
MOT
Nuts and Bolts check

The Alternator belt change was well timed as the existing one was found to be split. For the first time Boris failed his MOT due to a minor nick on the tele-lever ball joint gator so that had to be replaced too. He sailed through his re-test.

Left to Right – Harry, Cee-Jay and Craig

Racin n Cruisin had a new helper Harry Mann. Harry is 80 years old and was the mechanic for his Manx GP riding brother Ronnie. A great addition, I am sure.

I took a ride up to Braemar and camped overnight to make sure all was well. Another excellent destination and campsite to add to my favourites list. Boris was ready to go.

Roddy from MotoFreight contacted me advising me to apply for an Environmental Protection Agency permit to allow Boris (classed as dangerous goods) into the USA. He included sample copies and, in the end, it was a straight forward process to apply by email. A couple of weeks later the document arrived back by email. I now had all documentation required for the trip. I informed Roddy I had the permit so a pick-up date of the 11th of August was confirmed. It would be a cost of £185 to get Boris down south. I reckoned that this was well worth it.

I was aware that Graham, whom I had met on the Russian trip was going back to do the infamous Road of Bones. This is a stretch of unpaved road in the far east of Russia leading to Magadan. It was constructed in the Stalin era by Gulag prisoners – many of whom died in the process. It was famously featured in the Long Way Round TV series. I had offered to meet up again with Graham in mid-June but he informed me he was heading off on Monday June 17th to Russia. His plan was to ride his bike to Moscow, fly to Vladivostok then take a hire bike on the Road of Bones. He would then fly back to Moscow and meet his wife for a holiday, followed by a long and varied ride home. He sent through a picture that first morning of his bike fully loaded and ready to go. We would then exchange the occasional message on his progress. His last message to me was sent on July 2nd telling me excitedly that he was entering the Road of Bones. I messaged him on the 17th of July asking if all was well. After no reply I tried again on the 23rd and 25th of July. I was aware he would probably be out of contact for some time in such a remote area. I discussed it with Hutch and he suggested I check in with Alex from Rusmototravel. On August 1st I messaged Alex and he replied "Sadly Graham crashed on the Road of Bones." This did not sound good so I did some internet searching and to my horror discovered Graham died after colliding with a tanker. I was shocked and saddened to learn that on the brink of his 70th birthday this husband, father and grandfather had lost his life. I did not know Graham for long but in our short time together we had connected and I am sure we would have had many adventures together.

Graham's death hit me hard. I guess sharing the same passion with the same enthusiasm you cannot help but feel you are part of the same tribe. Suddenly he is gone while doing the thing he loved. I thought about the fear I had sensed in him about not being fit for adventures in the future. I guess one outcome is he will not have to face that now. He lived adventure, he died adventure.

It does not make me want me to give up motorcycle travel, but it does make me consider what type of travel I should do. People keep saying a ride across the USA should be a breeze in comparison to previous rides. Technically that should be true, but you still need to be careful and hope that luck remains with you. I always respond to those remarks with "hopefully so" and touch wood.

I attended Graham's funeral near Aberdeen. I thought about riding up on Boris but I feared it might upset his family. There was a message on the online post for the funeral stating it was a celebration of life so dress brightly. I misinterpreted that and wore bright t-shirt and casual trousers. Everyone else was dressed in formal wear with bright ties. I felt a bit embarrassed but took comfort in the thought that Graham would be laughing at me. It was a beautiful service with a loving family. I decided to skip the drinks and snacks based on my clothing choice.

Graham and I in Glencoe

"Rest in peace Amigo."

Let the Trip continue

On a rainy Sunday evening Boris was picked up as promised by MotoFreight. The first travel element of Once around the Block Part 2 was underway.

Monday 26/08/19

It was a 3:30am rise for Amber and I as the flight had a 6.05am departure. I was calm, excited and anxious all at the same time. We knew the M8 was closed as we made our way out to Glasgow Airport. We were relieved to find the diversion was quick and straight forward. Before long we pulled into the drop off area and hugged and said our good byes. "Don't die," Amber said. "I will do my best not to," I replied.

The check-in was easy and I zoomed through security. I was able to go to the executive lounge having a KLM status earned through 7 years of grueling work travel. You can imagine my delight to find they did bacon rolls. I am sure this is a Glasgow only offering. The flight was on time and trouble free. I moved swiftly through the terminals at Amsterdam Schiphol and boarded the SFO flight straight away, I had a great seat with unlimited legroom as it was located next to the exit door. The flight was 10 hours but with three movies and a sleep it passed quickly enough.

After arriving on time there was a big queue at immigration taking about an hour to get through. I was surprised this tech savvy city did not have the electronic clearance available elsewhere in the US. Once clear, I picked up my bag and headed out into the hot sunshine for a taxi. Within 10 minutes the taxi pulled up at the Virgin Freight building.

The lady behind the desk created a document and sent me around to the opposite side of the building to US Customs. The Customs folks were very friendly and processed me quite quickly. MotoFreight had advised me to ask for a 7501 or 3461 form which is needed to ship the bike back out. The Customs guys said I didn't need it. I was too tired and hot to argue. I took the document back round to the freight office where they told me all that was needed now was an $85 fee. Not a problem except they would only accept a company check or money order. Thankfully and quite bizarrely there was a Post Office located in the middle of this industrial estate within walking distance.

After payment I was sent to the warehouse to pick up the bike. "Where is your truck," the young warehouse guy asked. I showed him my screwdriver and said "I'm riding it out." He smiled and looked very surprised so I guess it's not a common occurrence. They had trouble finding the crate but eventually they delivered it to me. I had hoped they might help me unpack it but they showed no interest. Sixteen screws may not sound like a lot but when they are quite long, tight, on the bottom of a crate and you are overheated, it was exhausting.

I finally got them all out and wrestled the cover off. Just at that point a guy started chatting to me which was perfect timing as I needed a little help to push it off the pallet. The screen and mirrors had been removed but with rush hour looming I decided to ride out as is and I would sort them out at Marks house.

Boris being unpacked at SFO

I pulled out onto the road and was happy to see the tyre pressures did not need adjusting and my fuel was good for the journey ahead. The ride to Marks house was only 20 minutes and before long I was pulling up outside his door. It was great to see the big guy again and in true Mark style the first thing he did was drop my helmet from chest height with a bang on his tiled kitchen floor.

The house was like a Tardis, small on the outside and multi-story inside. There was a view of the bay which at that very moment was being consumed by Bay Area fog. I was given an en-suite room with its own entry at the bottom of the house. It was perfect. Mark told me to do my own thing and come up for dinner at 6:30pm.

I had a great time getting showered and sorting out my gear. The cooling from the fog also made for a pleasant environment to reinstate my mirrors and screen. I joined the guys for dinner meeting Mark's partner Russ and son Douglas. We had a good relaxing dinner getting to know each other. I headed off around 8pm to grab some much-needed sleep.

Tuesday 27/08/19

As expected, I had an erratic sleep but overall, I got enough rest. I went up to the house around 6:30am as requested and joined the guys for toast and delicious hot coffee. Douglas was like a half-shut knife, typical of a teenager getting ready for school. I asked Mark what his plans were, making it clear he had no obligation to show me around. He invited me to take a ride around town on our motorcycles, which suited me to a tee. Mark had recently bought a 2007 R1200GS which looked in excellent condition.

We started off by fuelling up then headed down to south San Francisco. Mark took the lead and I soon realised he did not use indicators. It made for an interesting guessing game at each junction. We stopped off by a beach where surfers were enjoying the waves. Mark took a photo of Boris and I with the Pacific Ocean in the background. Another major milestone. The bay was still fog bound but atmospheric. I asked Mark to use his turn signals to make life easier for me and safer for him. Mark being

Mark then moved into an occasional use, sometimes turning in the opposite direction, combined with hand signals. At one junction he was indicating one way and pointing the other way. I had to smile and keep guessing.

After riding through Golden Gate Park, we stopped off at a national park shop where I picked up an annual pass at a cost of $80. We would have had great views of the bridge had it not been for the fog. From there we moved on through Fort Mason (aptly named) and had a break for coffee. Mark had mentioned that he wanted to ride with me for a bit. I had taken that as today's ride but discovered he meant on the trip east. There was no way I would say no but part of me was a little disappointed that I was not heading out on my own. It was my issue, not Marks as he is a top guy. He told me he was thinking we could ride together to Arches National Park then I would head north to the Salt Lake City and he would head south to Santa Fe. That would mean 4 days together which would work well. I had not planned to take in Arches, but my plans were flexible.

We then went along past all the piers and through the city and onto a camping store to pick up a gas canister. From there we took the highway home. It was a great tour covering many areas I had not seen before.

After a brief lunch stop, we headed out to the airport to try and get the missing forms from customs. It was the same guy and he was adamant that the form given (3299) was the correct form for my circumstances. He would not issue another document but did give me a copy of the 3299. Let's see next year. Worst case, Canada here I come.

I had a quiet evening organising my luggage and had dinner with the guys. Another early night was had as I headed off to bed around 9pm. They had been great hosts and I had enjoyed my time with them.

Wednesday 28/08/19

I woke up to another foggy morning. I wandered up to the house for coffee and toast then set about packing the bike. I did a quick check with Mark to make sure he had all the required gear. It turned out he had no sleeping mat. I told him he would be really uncomfortable so he borrowed Russ's Yoga mat. As planned, we set off at 9:30am and did about a mile before Mark had to turn around and go back for his wallet.

Mark took an alternative route as Highway 101 was backed up, dropping us back on the highway just before the Bay bridge. The south bound traffic routes across the top with our north bound route built under it almost like a tunnel effect. I could see the top of Alcatraz to my left but not much else. After lots of busy suburban traffic we eventually emerged into the flat lush Sacramento valley and with it the hot sunshine.

We pulled over just before Sacramento for gas and coffee. Interestingly, the Starbucks also sold draft beer - can't say I've seen that before. We were soon on route 50 which at this point was still highway, eventually turning into a nice twisty "A" road all the way into Lake Tahoe. As it was mid-afternoon, we both agreed we should put in some more miles.

We eventually pulled up in to a Nevada town named Fallon. I had noticed the skies were darkening and I was sure a storm was close. I suggested to Mark we find a hotel and call it a day. We were getting towards 300 miles on day one and the temperature was 100 degrees. He happily agreed.

We checked into the Quality Inn and took some time out to get cleaned up and chill. We then wandered a few hundred yards to a local restaurant for Santa Fe burgers and garlic fries. Mark was amazed at the value for money versus San Francisco. This little desert town was a long way from big city life and prices. Perfect ending to a great first day.

Tuesday 29/08/19

The dimly lit clock showed 4:15am as I conceded I could not sleep any longer. Still I was quite content sorting stuff out in my room and doing some social media. I headed downstairs for a very basic breakfast at 5:30am, joining a couple of construction workers and a cowboy. I sat in the corner listening to their chat. They were all heading home for the labour day weekend.

After breakfast I walked down the quiet street to a Safeway store. I was looking for a small tin of coffee but Americans don't normally do small so I walked away empty handed. I was surprised to find slot machines in a Safeway store - welcome to Nevada. As I walked back into the hotel, I overheard the receptionist talk about how her husband was in prison for two years - welcome to Nevada.

I spotted Mark out at his bike. I asked him if he would like to leave earlier than the planned 8am departure to which he replied "I'm ready." So, by 7:30am we were on the road. We were in high desert wilderness in minutes with mountains looming in the distance. The route was stunning and continued to be all day. Massive tracts of empty land in-between small towns. Long movie set straights with curvy summit passes. We stopped to look at the pony express trail which was impressively clear. We had coffee in a small western town named Austin with a delightfully grumpy lady owner. Best of all I picked up a highway 50 sticker. You know by now I love a sticker.

We rode on all the way to Delta, Utah before the 407 miles covered in 90-degree heat took its toll and screamed no more. We agreed a hotel was appropriate and took the advice of a gas station employee to choose the Days Inn. Dinner that night was a Mexican next to the hotel which turned out to be probably the worst Mexican meal I have ever experienced. Still the chat was good and the beer was cold.

Friday 30/08/19

I was first in line for the basic breakfast provided by the hotel before we set off at 7:30am. We had a shorter ride today to Moab situated next to the Arches National Park. I had no expectations of the ride but boy was I in for a treat. Utah had been quite green farmland where we were but that all changed after a hundred miles or so. Just before getting to the more interesting terrain I noticed a sign saying "No services for 104 miles." I glanced at my fuel and saw I had 107 miles left. These models have notoriously bad fuel gauges so there was no way I could take the risk. I waved and sounded the horn to no avail as Mark had his earphones in listening to music. I finally caught up with him on the ramp to the interstate, passing him to pull him over. He had missed the sign and was down to a similar level of fuel as me. We u-turned on the one-way ramp and gingerly made our way back.

All fuelled up we hit one of the best interstate experiences I have had. Miles of red rock mountains, desert and canyons. It was spectacular. We pulled over to a view point and got chatting to three friendly guys on Harley's from Nevada. It got me thinking of my ex workmate Windy who is a big Harley guy. His club had arranged a motorcycle rally on the east coast of Scotland and Windy was given the job of leading the ride out. With something like 80 Harley's following him, Windy missed the turn off to Eyemouth harbour resulting in 80 hairy bikers doing a U-turn in a small housing estate. He was mortified.

We rode on and passed the Arches State Park just outside of Moab, as we wanted to arrange accommodation first. Again, I would have loved to camp but it was blisteringly hot. We found the River Canyon Lodge which was reasonably priced for this town and very nice. We had a great lunch in town waiting for our rooms to get ready. I told Mark I was going to take a risk and ride in T-shirt and shorts around the park. He happily bought into that plan, so that afternoon we carefully headed to the park which was spectacularly beautiful. For me it was the whole experience of the rock formations and colours. The Arches themselves were great but not the main event. Despite our casual dress I was still roasted, riding bandy legged to stop burning my legs on the bike. We did one short hike up to an arch which was impressive but soon after headed back to the hotel.

Arches National Park - Utah

Mark chilled out at the pool while I walked into town and had a couple of cold beers in Eddie McStiffs chatting to a young couple from Arizona. Utah restrict the alcohol content of draft beer to 3.1% which worked for me as I don't like strong beer. Later on, Mark and I walked to the same place for Tacos and another couple of beers.

Saturday 31/08/19

And then there was one.

My plan for the day was an early visit to Canyonlands then head north. Mark had decided to do the Canyonlands run too. It was a nice ride up and I was delighted to have clocked up $60 worth of my $80 National Park pass. Only one more to go and I was ahead.

The park was beautiful as expected with the bonus of curvy roads. We rode to the end where there was a spectacular outlook, then took the other fork to another view-point. A couple of guys were setting off on a hike, one of them with a holster complete with a revolver. This country is very strange. We came from Nevada where anything goes such as drugs, prostitution and gambling; to its neighbour Utah where draft beer is limited to 3.1% abv. Amazingly both let you go hiking tooled up.

We stopped off at the junction where we would part. Big Mark thanked me saying he had a brilliant time. I thanked him for his company too. He is a great lad and I enjoyed our time together. He hoped to be in Scotland for next year's Fringe Festival so we would catch up then. Last time I saw him ride away was in Novosibirsk, Siberia along with Graham. Oh, how fate deals a hand. I always feel a mix of sadness, excitement and fear when I break out on my own. This was no different.

The initial ride up through Nevada was boring interstate, followed by Colorado farm lands then industry scarred undulating desert. Eventually the road got more interesting winding up over mountains. It was over 90 degrees and was really uncomfortable but I pressed on. I re-entered Utah and had a brief stop at a gas station for pizza and coffee. My destination had been Vernal, Utah but it was still fairly early so I set my sights on Rock Springs, Wyoming. Vernal was clean cut but did not have much character so I was glad I had made that decision.

The ride between Vernal and Rock Springs was the best of the day as it was cooler and the green scenery made for a pleasant change. My bum was sore though and I was tired. Eventually I pulled into the Holiday Inn and was glad to shower and chill. I spent that night in the bar restaurant next door observing the locals getting excited over a Wyoming football match.

Sunday 01/09/19.

Last night I had a talk with myself. I need to slow down and make sure I enjoy the trip. I have plenty of time to reach Boston. I decided I would take full advantage of the Holiday Inn and have a short afternoon ride to somewhere below the parks. My logic was that on this Labour day weekend they will be busy Sunday but emptying out on Monday. I used the iOverlander app to identify a campsite in Pinedale just over 100 miles north. The campsite, which was a field in the middle of town, had no facilities other than a Porto-loo at a cost of $10 - perfect.

Before leaving Rock Springs I have some interesting facts. Butch Cassidy got his nickname while he was working as a butcher there. Another famous resident was Calamity Jane. A darker side of its history was the racist massacre of at least 28 Chinese miners who were perceived to be stealing the white communities' jobs.

The ride up was hot and mainly rolling open range but I could see mountains in the distance. I stopped off at a historical marker where I could see the wagon wheel ruts on the Oregon trail. I could not imagine how hard that would have been. I guess a bit of scary excitement.

Pinedale was a nice frontier town and when I found the camping field, I was happy with my choice. It was empty so I decided to head off to the Museum of the Mountain Men which I enjoyed and I had the bonus of cooling off.

The campsite set up was based on honesty. Fill in some details on an envelope, put in $10, take a flag, write the number on the envelope and deposit it in a box. It worked a treat. I set up camp only to discover my sleeping mat was missing. I searched high and low but to no avail. I just hope I forgot it and I haven't misplaced it on my travels. A bit ironic that I had been nagging Mark about his. It turned out that I had indeed forgot to bring it.

I walked into town and had dinner at the Wind River brewing company. I had been thinking about my trip ending and I had thought it would be nice to ride in with another few bikers. I had been considering posting a message on Facebook in the ex-Digital employees site asking if there was interest. I was a bit apprehensive but decided to go for it. That night I wrote:

Hi are there any Boston area Digital bikers out there who would like to join me on the final short leg of my motorcycle ride around the world (Once around the Block). All being well I will leave from the Mill at 10am on Sunday 14th Sep riding to my final destination of New England Aquarium. So far, I have finished all my big trips alone and while this time my wife will be waiting for me at the destination, it would be nice to ride in with one or two bikers. Please pm me if you are Interested for further details. — in Pinedale, Wyoming.

I thought I would be bound to get at least a few hairy guys in Harley's interested.

Monday 02/09/19

I awoke early and went out to use the toilet. It was freezing and I was totally unprepared with my warm layers still in the bike. I lay in my sleeping bag and watched a downloaded episode of "The West" which I thought was appropriate. When the sun came up, I started packing and had another failed search for my sleeping mat. I noticed that another camper had arrived after I had gone to sleep last night. I gave him a wave as I headed into town for breakfast. Thankfully a place opened at 7am although my rancher's skillet was pretty awful. At least I had coffee and I was able to warm-up. I checked on last night's Facebook post and had received quite a lot of supportive comments many from my Scottish ex colleagues but no takers so far. Still, it was early days.

I made my way out of town still feeling cold. I stopped to zip up my air vents and switched on the heated grips. The heat gradually started to come through as the sun rose higher. The ride was relatively short and soon I was in Jackson. The unintentional priority of the day was to find a Walmart with a cheap sleeping pad. Sadly, Jackson being a designer mountain town did not have a Walmart or a sleeping pad under $60. I noticed a Staples and had a brainwave. I would buy a roll of bubble wrap and make my own.

I left Jackson complete with a roll of bubble-wrap strapped to my bag. Not long out of Jackson the Grand Tetons in all their splendour emerged. I was in National Park number 3 and $10 to the good on my park pass. I was a little worried I might not get a camping spot so I headed straight to Coulter Bay. The route took me along the base of the Tetons to my left and fairly flat lands to the right. The Tetons rise to 13,755 feet which pales the 3000 plus feet of the Cullin's in Skye into insignificance... but the plains are already at 6237 feet so the Tetons actually appear to be similar. As impressive as they are, I love where I live.

I arrived at Coulter Bay and was relived to find they had plenty of space. The guy charged me $24 for two nights and directed me to a hiker/biker site. Apparently, my park pass gave me a discount and I had also turned up on day 1 of low season. I had expected it to cost $70. The site was perfect, set in the woods with a picnic bench and bear box. The guy told me that there was a black bear around but she was timid.

I set up camp and got the bike gear off and rode in my shirt and shorts down to the main area to check it out. There were a couple of shops, a restaurant and a visitor centre. I bought a lunch snack and headed back to the tent site. Later on, I returned and spent some time in the visitor centre then picked up food and firewood to take back. It was too good a pitch not to use.

The guy from the couple on the next pitch came over to say hi. They were from South Dakota and were touring around on their Polaris trikes. After relaying to him the story about my missing mat he told me he had spotted cheap ones in the shop onsite. This I had to check out.

Teton National Park – Wyoming

Tuesday 03/09/19

My makeshift mat was better than hard ground but not great, leading to another uncomfortable sleep. It was cold but not as bad as yesterday. I made some coffee and soon after headed off. My plan was to spend the morning in Jackson then take a slow ride through the park.

I stopped off on the way at an old simple log ranch dwelling with incredible views. This rancher had originally fought against the formation of the park but in later years became a big supporter.

I stopped off outside a tourist information centre, stripped off the bike gear and locked my helmet to the crash bar. First priority was a breakfast which I found down a side street for a reasonable cost. I sat outside in the sunshine watching the world go by while reading the local Jackson free press. It was bliss.

I noticed there was a free town walking tour at 10:30am so I joined that. It was an interesting tour, apart from the usual participants who wanted to talk more about themselves rather than letting the guide do his job. Afterwards I did a bit of souvenir shopping then headed off.

I meandered slowly through the park stopping off at viewpoints, eventually returning back to my pitch to chill. I headed down to the store and sure enough there was a $15 sleeping mat which I grabbed straight away.

I walked down later to the bar and had a very American starter platter which filled me up. On my way back I noticed that another GS had filled a spot. He was English living in the US. We exchanged stories then I moved on. I had a new neighbour who had a Harley. I heard him talking away but could not see the other person. I soon realised there was no other person, he was talking loudly to himself. Hmm I thought, I am neighbours with a guy in a gun crazy state who talks to himself enthusiastically and loudly. Not ideal.

A little while later the guy approached me. He said "sorry you might hear me talk to myself, too much time on the road." I smiled and said "no worries." He was from Canada and was fascinated by my bike. We shook hands and off he went. Within a few minutes I could hear him chatting away. Time for bed.

Wednesday 04/09/19

I had a great sleep on my cheap mat. What a difference! I made some coffee, packed up, then headed down to the general store for a banana. I routed north towards Yellowstone and stopped off for breakfast soon after entering the park. It was an idyllic experience, overlooking a lake, with friendly staff and was great value.

I had been in Yellowstone before but planned to loop around the park before exiting east. I stopped off at Old Faithful only to find it was an hour and ten minutes from doing its thing. I moved on.

I was enjoying the ride and since I had been there before I was free of having to stop at all of the points of interest. It was warm so when I found myself in a roadworks queue that could last up to 30 minutes I bailed out and headed for the exit.

Heading for the exit still meant a ride of probably 70 miles passing herds of buffalo, crystal clear lakes and over a mountain pass. Once out, I had another 100 or so miles to ride to my destination of Greybull. I stopped off at the visitor centre in Cody which other than air conditioning had little of interest.

After a hot 50 miles ride over the arid plains I arrived at the Historic Hotel in Greybull. It did feel very western and a little creepy as I was the only one there. There were various long corridors and all the bedroom doors lay open. I could just imagine them all slamming shut in the dead of the night.

I had a shower, sorted my gear out and headed out in search of food. I had read a little guide in the room that suggested the adjoining restaurant did great Wyoming steak. I thought I might treat myself. I had also read there were three western saloons in town. Two were smoking and one was not. I asked downstairs if the restaurant was open and was told yes, tomorrow.

I wandered around the little town and found the non-smoking saloon. It was a very traditional run-down bar with a few old guys and some painters still in their whites hanging around. The bar person was a loud friendly black woman who welcomed me and explained the beer choices, which I was amazed to see was more than Budweiser and Coors. I asked for a pint of the local ale. "You sure you don't want a four-and-a-half-pint pitcher, it's better value?" I stuck to my pint at a time strategy. An old guy became my best friend immediately after hearing my accent. He told me about his fiery Irish wife, his career in mining and his petrol head addiction. I asked if they served food. "Sure, they do," he replied directing the bar lady to put on the special pizza for me. It was the equivalent of a supermarket pizza from the value section, but it was food. He told me I should take route 14 over the Bighorn mountains and I would not regret it. I told him I would. I left fairly early satisfied that I'd had a good night, although I should have listened to the bar lady and took the pitcher.

Thursday 05/09/19

Breakfast was a little help yourself corner in reception. I had some toast, bananas and was ready for the road. I had about 90 miles of fuel left so I wondered if I should top up. I had noticed Shell was the next town 20 miles up the road. Shell had to be the place to fill up.

As I entered Shell, I read the usual American sign advising the elevation and population. With only 87 of a population I immediately assumed they would not have a Gas Station. I was correct which put me on edge as I had barely enough to reach the big town of Sheridan ahead. I slowed right down to conserve fuel, which was good in a way as the road became spectacular. The ride up was cutting through deep red canyons with the bighorn river beside me negotiating hairpin bends. The road gradually climbed up over the mountain pass.

Once on top, the countryside became more fertile and I was halted by cowboys herding cattle. I started to take a picture but I was told in no uncertain terms it was not wanted. I enjoyed watching these guys on horseback accompanied by a few scraggy dogs controlling their herd.

The trip down the mountain was steep sweeping bends which were a joy to ride. At the bottom there was a petrol station.

I soon joined Interstate 90 and started the long ride towards Sturgis. I stopped off after a while and had some burritos and air conditioning. A good distance further on when I stopped to refuel, I got talking to a biker who advised me to take another road off the highway. A little further down the road I cut off and took a longer side road. Just at the cut off I stopped at Donna's Diner for a bowl of chilli and some lemonade. It was full of retirees with Donna commanding the place. Proper old school American.

The first half of the detour was same scenery, longer road. I eventually reached the town of Newcastle which was the entry point into the Black Hills. Thankfully, the riding and scenery changed from flat and brown to green, hilly and curvy.

I had been looking at accommodation in Sturgis and noticed Deadwood also had some decent prices. My route would take me through Deadwood and on into Sturgis, so I could suss out both. Deadwood was very pretty and very touristy but still quite appealing. I spied the Hilton branded hotels I had identified and they were in a decent location at a reasonable price. As planned, I pressed on to Sturgis for a look around town. I spotted the Indian Motorcycle Dealer just as I rode in so I stopped off for a look. It was a cracking dealership and they directed me to a campsite on the edge of town. They also told me there would be some Super Moto street racing this weekend. I had no notion of camping after such a long ride so I opted to go back and spend the night in Deadwood followed by a couple of nights camping in Sturgis.

Boris in Sturgis - South Dakota

I was glad to finally park up Boris and get checked into what was quite a nice hotel, apart from the casino below it. I don't like casinos. As usual I sorted out my gear then took a walk into the historic Main Street. I wandered into Wild Bills bar only to discover that was where he was shot in the back of the head during a card game. I had a nice beer there before moving on a few doors to a burger joint. I called in to Wild Bills on the way back and took the barman's recommendation to try Wild Bill Ale, brewed in the old way. It was horrible.

Friday 06/09/19

I had a plan. Go do my laundry (big priority), go pitch my tent in Sturgis then go visit Mount Rushmore and Crazy Horse monument. It was overcast and cool as I stepped out that morning. I rode a mile or so to Deadwood Station Bunkhouse and Casino, which also had a laundromat.

It was early, empty and ideal. I sipped on the free coffee and read the magazines quite contentedly. A Harley pulled up with a husband and wife who were also there to do laundry. The guy, who runs a motorcycle shop in Upper New York State chatted away to me. He gave me some good advice on the ethanol content in most American petrol. He told me as long as I am running the bike no problem but do not leave it sitting with that type of fuel over a winter in Boston. He also advised me that I should add a fuel treatment.

I headed back to the hotel complete with clean clothes and checked out. There was a spit of rain in the air as I headed back to Sturgis. The campsite could not be described as pretty but it was functional and at $11 a night very affordable. I pitched up on the hardest ground on the planet then headed off down the interstate Black-hills bound.

Once off the interstate the road and scenery were excellent with green forested rolling hills. Before long I was riding into Mount Rushmore. Having seen it many times on TV, I knew what to expect and it was impressive. It was a big tourist operation with multi story car parks and designated trails. Unfortunately, restoration work was going on in front of the mountain which detracted from its grandeur a little. I took a path above the works which gave me an uninterrupted view. I was left feeling a bit confused. Was it right to blow up a beautiful mountain to create this? I am not so sure.

The ride to the Crazy Horse memorial was nice and to be honest I enjoyed it better than Mt Rushmore. I loved the story of how the old Indian, Henry Standing Bear asked Korczak Ziolkowski who had been working on Mt Rushmore to create a version to honour Native Americans. The difference is they wanted to do it without government money and create additional legacies such as a university. The work started in 1948 and is a long way from finished. Only the face has been created of the final warrior on a horse. Ziolkowski died but his family members keep it going, still refusing government funding.

The visitors centre was a big museum with the usual food and retail elements. My father would have been in his glory and could have spent 2 days there where I did 2 hours. They offered rock from the site to take away. I took one for me and one for my father, which I will place by his grave. He would like that.

I took the scenic route back to Sturgis stopping off at Deadwood Cemetery to visit the graves of Wild Bill and Calamity Jane. Apparently, Calamity had a thing for Wild Bill and her dying wish was to be buried beside him. She got her wish but I'm not sure how Wild Bill would have felt about it.

Once back in Sturgis I wandered into town and had a look around before selecting the Knuckle Saloon for food and beer. It was a huge place with a long bar filled with hairy old bikers. I enjoyed it. I have observed that although there is a wide variety of local craft beers, I seemed to be the only one drinking them. Budweiser is still king in the states.

The walk was longer than I realised, which I felt especially on the way home in need of a pee!

Saturday 07/09/19

A chilling day in greater Sturgis. First on the agenda was a visit to McDonalds to get Wi-Fi and try to catch Amber who was visiting my Mother. I sent a message saying I was around and sure enough the FaceTime call came in. It was good to catch up.

Next up was the Sturgis Motorcycle Museum which was really good. Lots of nice old Indian bikes. I then visited the museum of US Cavalry at Fort Mead where the 7th Cavalry had been positioned after their defeat at the Little Big Horn. It was good but I felt as if I was in the museum of my rival team. I far preferred the Crazy Horse Museum.

I then visited the Indian Motorcycle dealer followed by the BMW Shop.

Later on, I walked back into town to take in the Super Moto. These guys are seriously nuts but entertaining to watch. I also noticed the US rules around spectator safety must be quite different. There were lots of people in direct line of fire positioned behind flimsy fences.

112

For dinner I ended up in the same place (The Knuckle Saloon) sitting next to the same old guy at the bar. I was becoming a local.

Sunday 08/09/19

Wagons roll! It was a brighter morning than forecasted as I headed out of town early. I found a local restaurant on the edge of Deadwood for breakfast. I got talking to three Harley riders before going in and we had a good exchange of stories. The breakfast was proper American and just what I needed.

I headed south and took the famous Needles Highway, which makes its way through Custer State Park. It was a terrific ride with switchbacks, tunnels and super scenery. From there I did a big loop through the wildlife area and spotted some bison and deer. I stopped off at Custer for a look around. It was a typical little western tourist town. From there I headed south and eventually east to visit Wounded Knee the scene of the massacre of Big Foot and his followers.

The site consisted of a double-sided billboard telling the story and some open shacks with a couple of Native American ladies selling their wares. One of the ladies told me the massacre took place within a 5-mile radius of this site as people scattered in a panic. She pointed up to a small hill where the mass grave was located.

I had a couple of problems. My main one was I was ready for a pee but there was nowhere to go so I felt rushed. The second is deeper and bigger. I had just ridden 50 or so miles through the Oglala Lakota lands and it had been quite depressing with much of it populated with mobile homes. I was now at the last site of the last fight between the Lakota and the US Cavalry and it was so basic. My thoughts trouble me because maybe the culture wants it to be like this, but why then can such a great job be done at the Crazy Horse memorial. It was a tragedy that a race lost their way of life. I only wish they could move on and honour what they had in a positive way.

Wounded Knee could have a proper visitors centre telling the story of the atrocity, providing jobs and raising revenues for the people and most important of all, it should have a loo! Sounds better to me than the multitude of casinos now being developed on Native American lands.

I headed north towards Badlands and stopped off to pee as soon as I could find somewhere to hide. Badlands was so cool I decided to camp there. I paid $12 for a huge pitch on nice soft ground. I ate a delicious Sioux flatbread pizza in the park restaurant then took a ride through the park that night. It was great. I felt a little sad as I would be leaving the west behind.

Badlands National Park – South Dakota

Monday 09/09/19

It was a perfect campsite, quiet and peaceful and I slept like a log. It rained quite hard during the night but I stayed dry and cosy. I got up and made some coffee then took a walk to find out when the store opened. It turned out to be 8am so I had another coffee and chatted to an English biker neighbour now living in Canada.

I packed and rode up to the shop to pick up some presents. Satisfied with my purchases I moved on. Not much further up the road I visited a turf settler dwelling which was quite interesting. I loved the fact there were prairie dogs running around the site.

Ok so it's east on Interstate 90 and don't spare the horses. It was pretty boring and I was getting battered from a southernly wind. I kept straining my neck muscles to hold my helmet still.

I stopped off to eat then again to visit the Museum of the Sioux Nation, both of which were good. I made good progress and pulled into the Norwood Inn in Worthington, Minnesota for the night. I chatted to a couple with a Gold Wing from Myrtle Beach. They said it had been raining hard all day until I pulled up. Funnily enough I had come upon many wet roads but no rain. As Amber constantly reminds me, I am a lucky sod.

Tuesday 10/09/19

After what was the worst breakfast of the trip due to a smelly coughing woman, I was off again. I had put the Indian Motorcycle factory into my Garmin the night before and it was only 27 miles away. It involved a small southern detour but would be worth it. It was very rural but I eventually emerged in Spirit Lake and arrived at the factory soon after. I had written to them telling them my story and asking for a factory tour but they had replied advising they were not available at the moment due to construction.

As I parked up, I asked a lady if she could take some photos. She could not have been more helpful. Turns out she was the factory nurse. I went inside and explained my situation. The receptionist was pleasant and said "Give me a shout and I will switch on the 8-minute video that explains how the factory works." There were some nice bikes, both new and vintage and some apparel. Before long I watched the video. It certainly was the modern manufacturing facility I expected to see which was far flung from the Ural factory in Russia. I left feeling a little disappointed. Here was a guy from

Scotland riding around the world and an Indian customer. I could be perceived as thinking I am the great I am here but if someone had rocked up to my factory with this story, I'm sure I would have made them feel a bit special. Still I am glad I came but I did not buy a t-shirt.

The Factory – Spirit Lake

From there it was north and east. The wind had dropped but the temperature had risen. I was desperate to camp but there were thunderstorms forecast overnight so it did not make sense. I stopped in a rest area and got chatting to a photographer from Chicago. He was a nice gentle guy who had spent some time up in the Yukon photographing home nation people. We chatted about our shared love for that area. He gave me some hints and tips about the Chicago ride. We were soon joined by a Boston couple who had followed me in to the rest area to find out where I was from. They were on a big road trip and had visited many of the same places I had been. It was a nice chance encounter. The Boston couple were talking about danger and constant tolls and started to spook me little. They left and the Chicago fellow and I agreed people are generally good and tolls are a nuisance but not a disaster.

The ride was through endless flat corn fields until I crossed the border into Wisconsin, which greeted me with a Mississippi River crossing. I whooped for joy. Then for the next 10 miles or so there were lakes, hills and curves, finally settling down to straight, tree lined highway. I pulled into a cheap motel in Lake Delton to rest up for the night. It was one of those motels where there are overnighters at one end and long termers at the other. Lots of noisy old muscle cars and enquiring looks. I wandered out and had a delicious, cheap, authentic Mexican meal that night.

Wednesday 11/09/19

The cheap motel did not feel good. I had flies in my room but I managed to get rid of them by switching on the extra loud air con. I was glad to get going. My target was to get beyond Chicago, which at just under 200 miles away should be very do-able.

The weather was hot and humid and again I came upon wet roads just after the rain had gone. I approached my first toll and although it was awkward on a bike, the process was smooth. The traffic increased along with the number of lanes as I approached Chicago. There was roadworks that seemed to go on forever but the traffic kept flowing. The number of toll stops also increased which was a hassle. I was now effectively on motorway with service stations which allowed a break without a toll exit. I took a break just before the big push through Chicago.

Chicago suburbs lasted forever but the busy traffic was flowing. I thought to myself I must have passed the city by now and be on the east side. Out of the haze, way in the distance, the Chicago skyline emerged. At the same time the traffic slowed right down to 1st and 2nd gear pace. Thankfully it didn't stop but it was hard going in the intense heat. I rode through the heart of the city and as I emerged from the other side the pace picked up.

Before I knew it, I was in Indiana. I hadn't realised Indiana was so close to Chicago. My first ever trip to the US in 1983 was to my first wife's relatives in Crane Indiana . I was a young raw boy but was looked after by her uncle Cecil like a father while I was there. He is dead now but would have been younger than me at that time. The last time I entered the state was by greyhound bus and here I was 37 years later riding in on Boris.

The first toll stop was one where you pick up a ticket. I pressed the button and nothing happened. The traffic started piling up behind me. I frantically looked to see if I was missing something. I pressed the help button and a woman started talking to me but it was hard to hear her in all the traffic. Eventually a lady popped her head around and told me to hang on. A minute later she came back and got me a ticket. Nobody honked their horn or gave me any hassle but it was a pain in the heat. The next toll stop was unmanned, wouldn't take my card and rejected my dollars. I eventually got a $20 note to work and it gave me $15 change in coins. Why take the toll road you may ask. It was just a case of long days and uninteresting scenery made me want to make it as easy as possible.

I pulled into a service station and chilled for a while. The clouds were getting angry and I wanted a decent hotel that night, so I booked a Holiday Inn in Toledo. Bonus was I would get to sing "In a bar in Toledo." A guy approached me asking about my trip. Turns out he was from Ulaanbaatar in Mongolia. We chatted away for a while about the merits of big bikes versus small bikes. He was working as a truck driver and hoped to be going home soon.

I finally got some rain on the last part of the route but not that much. It was great to arrive after a 400 plus miles day. Shower, change, eat then beer with footage of 9/11 showing in the bar. Took me back to that very day as I walked out of my office in Brussels to be told of what was happening. Sobering thought.

I called Tracy my ex colleague to confirm arrangements for Boris storage. I had proposed I drop it off the next Wednesday and another ex-colleague, Bob Moore had agreed to meet me there, he would take me back to Boston and we would have dinner with our wives. Tracy was good with the plan. He told me he likely had to travel next week so he would probably miss me. We would catch up next year. He asked me what my ride in plans were? I told him I still planned Sunday but Saturday was a possibility. What I didn't say was I had no takers to ride in with me and I thought, why wait just outside of Boston to ride in alone when I can do it on Saturday night.

Thursday 12/09/19

I took it easy that morning as I knew Amber was flying and she might be in touch. Sure enough the message popped up "the flight from Glasgow is 40 minutes late." I assured her all would be fine and eventually it took off 30 minutes late. Next message relayed the fact it had landed but was taking forever to get to the gate. I checked her next flight and gate and let her know it was still not boarding so all was well. I confirmed it was a long walk but there was no security to go through. I finally got a text saying I'm onboard. Time to ride.

What I thought was a very direct route turned out not to be. The Sat Nav was trying to send me off the highway when I knew that was the direct route. I came to a split in the highway and took the wrong fork. I'm convinced route 90 was not sign-posted but I am sure I could be proved wrong. The weather was overcast and cooler but still the ride was long. I eventually figured out my error and took a 50-mile hike north to get back on track. I followed the Sat Nav for the final 30 miles or so and it led me on a crazy traffic ridden route through a grubby Buffalo. I was glad to get to the hotel.

The hotel was cheap but alright and in a perfect location for the falls. For the first time since San Francisco, I removed the Sat Nav and put the cover on the bike. There were too many people hanging around. I talked to Amber on the phone as she had landed safely and made it to her hotel. I told her I was a little ahead of schedule and I may arrive Saturday. She was fine with that.

Many years ago, I had tried to persuade a work colleague, Peter Grant to make the 400 plus mile journey from Boston over a weekend to see the falls. "Why would I want to go all that way to see water running off a dyke?" he replied. Well, here I was some 30 odd years later looking at the water running off a dyke. It was powerful and impressive but the surroundings, route and traffic to get here took something away from the raw nature. Maybe Peter had a point. I would return in the morning.

That night I sat in the hotel bar listening to karaoke which was really varied and good. There were a couple of old guys who I would guess had been friends forever. I enjoyed just observing them catching up and laughing out loud. I have noticed whenever I stop for a break - from McDonalds to a Gas station café - there are often groups of old men socialising. It's nice to see.

Friday 13/09/19

I woke up feeling refreshed and the sunshine added to my more positive mood. I was first in line for the basic but welcomed breakfast. I had badly needed to do my laundry so I rode to a laundromat a couple of miles downtown. It was a 24-hour laundromat and at 8am there was just a guy, a lady and myself. Before long I was on my own and was at the drying stage when the door opened and a stocky guy burst in. He started cursing and swearing, muttering about his clothes still being wet. My danger sensors kicked in so I just sat quietly waiting on my dryer to finish. I decided to get up and do a confident check on my dryer and acknowledge him. He told me in colourful language not to use the washer he had used then thankfully he moved on.

I returned to the hotel and took a walk down to another viewing point for the falls. It was sunny and they looked impressive. I had planned to take the Maid of the Mist boat trip but the line of tourists following umbrellas put me off. I went back to the hotel, packed up and moved on. The ride through upper New York State was scenic. I made stops for food and fuel a couple of times and by early evening I entered Mass. I had hoped to stay at a hotel in the Westfield area 100 miles or so east of Boston but sadly the hotels were full or way overpriced. I checked closer to Boston and found a good deal at the Westborough Holiday Inn. The hotel was located on route 495 which was the main drag for Digital Equipment facilitates in my previous work life. It felt iconic taking that exit and after another 400 mile plus day with the sun setting, I pulled into the hotel.

There were Harley's parked everywhere as I approached the covered area just outside reception. I dismounted and said hi to three likely lads standing by their bikes. They all looked a bit surprised to see this pasty old biker rolling in on a BMW to their meet. I asked them what's happening and as usual the Scottish accent defused things. They told me it was a Harley Hells Angels meetup, which I had assumed by the colours worn on their backs. I briefly told them my story. One of the guys said (in his best Scottish accent) "So you're a BMW rider at an Angels meeting, as they say in Scotland "your fucked."" We all laughed and one of the guys handed me a miniature bottle of Glenlivet.

I decided not to wear my Indian t-shirt that night and kept a low profile. Any of the guys I came across were warm and friendly.

Saturday 14/09/19

I had identified a Walmart to pick up a fuel treatment as recommended by the guy back in Deadwood. I then fuelled up on the highest-grade fuel I could find. I would add the treatment and fill up just before dropping off the bike. I then rode as planned to the old Digital Equipment headquarters which was a converted mill in the very traditional small town of Maynard. I was feeling great as the Sat Nav routed me through lots of rural towns with scenery that brought back happy memories. The Mill has now been divided up into lots of small businesses including a Brew Pub. I had identified a street corner where the founder, Ken Olsen had a plaza named after him. It was across from Boston Bean House coffee shop where I had planned to meet up with other riders.

It's kind of weird to arrive at a place you had found using Google street view more than a year previous. I rode up onto the pavement and took a few pictures. I had agreed to meet Amber at 9:30am and my Sat Nav was showing an arrival time of 9:20am so I could not hang around. I coaxed a frightened looking guy to take a picture of me then I was off.

The route eventually joined highway 2 which offered up a great view looking down onto the city. I was riding very carefully as I did not want to blow it in my last few miles. I was held up a few times at road works so my arrival time was moving towards 9:30am. The weather was dry with light cloud and I was feeling on top of the world. I was within about a mile of my destination when I took a wrong turn which launched me onto the 5 lane I-

95 North. "Damn it!" I thought as I negotiated over the 5 busy lanes to exit and get back on track. I made it and it had only set me back by about 10 minutes or so. I was relieved to see that I was finally on the street heading towards the Aquarium.

I could see Amber in the distance so I rode to the end of the driveway and cheekily bumped up onto the paved area. We hugged and chatted and took some photos, which by chance had an American Flag painted Duck Boat behind us. Out of nowhere this enthusiastic young American guy came up to us and asked if I had seen the Long Way Round, his all-time favourite adventure show. When I told him, I had and that I had just completed my version of the trip, he was ecstatic. We chatted away and took photos. His name was Jobian Day and along with Amber they helped make my arrival feel special.

Amber, Boris the Duck Boat and I

505 days and 15,866 miles after setting off from Ardnamurchan Lighthouse (Scotland's most westerly point) I had reached

Boston. The US section had been epic, covering just under 5000 miles.

I had now ridden "Once around the block". Felt good!

Summary and Close

I rode Boris back to the hotel and parked him up in a good secure spot near reception. I went back out on him again on the Monday still pursuing the missing customs document. It felt like being in a video game, riding my own bike through the city traffic, in the sunshine. I really enjoyed it. Customs Boston agreed with Customs San Francisco that my document was fine as was. I agreed with MotoFreight that I would send a copy of it on my return and they would check it with their US broker.

On the Wednesday I took Boris to his winter home in Maynard. On the way I added the fuel treatment and topped the tank up. Kathy, the lady who was accommodating him was very nice. I connected the trickle battery charger and covered him up. I had meant to wash him but had been unable to find anywhere nearby. My old work mate, Bob Moore turned up as planned to give me a ride back into the city. It was great to catch up with him.

Once around the Block has been a brilliant experience with hard struggles - like the Gobi Desert - through to joyful rides - such as the Bighorn Mountain Pass. Splitting it into two parts had worked really well for me with the timing of both trips feeling just right. I had met many interesting people and made some new friends. I had also lost one in Graham.

My passion still burns for Motorcycle travel and I am already looking forward to riding the Appellations next year. Beyond that I have Australia in my sights. As long as I have the health I will keep on riding.

You can find posts and pictures from the trip on the Face Book group "Once around the Block by Motorcycle".

See you out there.

RIP Graham Vavangas (1949 – 2019). Our time together was short but you made an impact.

Printed in Poland
by Amazon Fulfillment
Poland Sp. z o.o., Wrocław